BLESS YOUR MESS BABY, BUT CLEAN IT UP NOW!

GRANDMA SNIFFA'S SASSY, SCIENCE AND PSYCHOLOGY BACKED WISDOM TO DRAG YOU OUT OF ROCK BOTTOM

SNIFFA S

First and foremost, I offer my deepest gratitude to Almighty Jesus, my guiding light, my healer, and my eternal source of strength. Without Your grace, this journey wouldn't have begun, and this book would never have been written. Every word is a reflection of the purpose You placed within me.

This book is lovingly dedicated to my kind and wise grandparents Maria Thires, Glory Bai, Chellan, and Savariar Adimai. To my amazing parents, Sheeba S and Siva Rajan your love, sacrifices, and unwavering belief in me are the foundation of everything I am. Heartfelt gratitude to Akshaya Ravichandran, my best friend celebrating 10 years of support, strength, and unconditional presence.

And lastly, to me Sniffa. For showing up. For staying consistent. For choosing growth even when it hurt. I'm proud of you.

With all my love and gratitude,
Sniffa

Contents

Acknowledgements   *vii*

Prologue   *ix*

Part 1

  1. Baby, Get Out Of The Mess   3

  2. It's Time To Take Ownership   17

  3. Take Responsibility For Your Actions   24

  4. Shifting Your Mindset From 'Why' To 'What'   31

  5. Cheat Your Mind And Set Yourself Free   37

  6. The Mind's Trick Mirror   44

  7. Don't Die With Your Light Still In You   48

Part 2

  8. The Strength In Stillness- Choosing Response Over Reaction   59

  9. Stress: Grandma's Wisdom On Turning Pressure Into Power   68

10. Faith – The Art Of Trusting Divine Timing   76

11. Take It One Day At A Time   83

12. The Mirage Of Satisfaction – The Art Of Being Content   88

13. Love Yourself Enough – The Science, The Spirit, The Stand   94

14. Embrace Your Flaws – The Radical Art Of Being Perfectly Imperfect 99

15. Treat Your Body Like A Temple   107

16. The Power Of Prayer- A Quiet Force That Changes Everything   112

Part 3

17. Be Kind   119

18. Be Honest, Love   125

19. The Art Of Coexisting   132

20. Never Underestimate The Power Of Having Good People Around You   138

21. People Skills -The Real Secret To Success   144

22. Giving: Grandma's Magic To Multiplying   150

Part 4

Contents

23. Gratitude, Baby: Grandma's Secret Spice   159

24. Spend Time With Nature   165

25. The Power Of Words- What You Say Can Save A Life   172

26. The Power Of Speed In Success   181

27. The Unshakeable Power Of Confidence   186

Part 5

28. The Future Is Calling You Back   197

29. We Never Meet Anyone By Accident   201

The End   205

Acknowledgements

My dearest, yes you holding this book in your hands:
Thank you for letting me be a part of your growth.
May these pages remind you of your strength, your light, and the love you've always deserved.
This isn't just a book, it's me, sitting beside you, having a conversation that matters.
From my heart to yours,
With so much love and honest truth, always.
Please write to me once you finish, I'd love to know how these pages found you when you needed them.
-Sniffa ?

PROLOGUE

"You Don't Need to Have It All Together to Begin, Sugar."

Precious one,

Well, look at you picking up this book in the middle of all life's noise and nonsense. I'm proud of you already. Because it takes guts, real guts, to decide you're ready for something better even when everything around you feels like a mess. Life doesn't always go the way you scribbled it down in your journal, does it? You give your all and still feel like you came up short. People you swore would stick around? Poof. Gone. And maybe just maybe your heart's been carrying a silent load no one else seems to notice. But sugar, let me tell you what someone should've told you a long time ago: You're allowed to fall apart. You're just not meant to stay there. Lean in close, baby, and listen good: how you see your situation makes all the difference. I've always said, the brightest stars are born in the darkest nights. Rock bottom? Honey, it's just the solid ground where you plant your feet and rise. The pressure you're under right now, it's real. But you've got two choices: let it bury you or let it build you. And the power to choose? That's sitting right in your pretty little hands.

Before we dive into the deep stuff in this book, I want to tell you a story that's older than my favourite teacup and ten times as important. It's from Socrates, a man who knew a thing or two about wisdom. So, one day, this fella asks Socrates, "How do I get wise?" And Socrates, being the sassy genius he was, tells him, "Meet me at the river tomorrow." The man shows up, expecting some grand answer. Instead, Socrates shoves his head under the water and holds it there! The poor man's flailing like a fish, desperate to breathe. Finally, Socrates lets him up and asks, "What did you want the most while you were down there?" "Air," he gasps. And Socrates, cool as ever, says, "When you want wisdom as much as you wanted that air, you'll find it." Now that, sugar, is the kind of hunger you need for change. You've gotta want growth so bad that you're willing to get uncomfortable for it. Get out of your little bubble. Stretch your heart and your habits. That's where the magic lives. I get asked all the time by bright eyed students, "Grandma Sniffa, how do I find happiness?" And I always say the same thing: willingness is half the battle. The rest? Well, it's just rolling up your sleeves and doing the work.

This book? It's not a magic wand. It's a mirror and a toolbox. And how much it helps you depends entirely on how deep you're willing to dig. Some chapters might sting a little, they're supposed to. Growth isn't always graceful, but it sure is worth it. J.D. Jakes said it best: *"If you always do what you've always done, you'll always be where you've always been."* That's why flipping pages alone won't change your life. You've gotta live these lessons, not just read them. Think of it like learning to drive, reading the manual won't get you anywhere unless you get in the car and hit the gas. Each principle in here is a little seed. And you, sweetheart, are the gardener. Plant them right, water them daily, and soon enough, you'll be walking through fields of your own becoming. You want peace? Clarity? Purpose? Then you've got to feed your mind like it's your best friend. Because here's the truth: your mind believes what you tell it. Every single day. So feed it love, hope, and bold belief in what's possible. This book will show you how to do just that. One shift at a time.

By the time you turn the last page, I hope you see yourself the way I already do, stronger than your pain, wiser than your past, and worthy of the peace you've been chasing. You've got a light in you, baby. This book is just here to help you turn it back on. So don't rush. Take your time. And know I'm cheering for you, every step of the way. Now let's begin, love. Grandma's got your back.

With all my heart,
Grandma Sniffa

The Awakening -Getting Out of the Fog These chapters help the reader recognize the mess, take ownership, and shift perspective.

I
Baby, Get Out of the Mess

"The mind in its own place and in itself can make a heaven of hell and a hell of heaven." – John Milton

Now listen here, sweetheart. I want you to understand why this chapter is sitting right at the front, bold and unapologetic. Imagine you're standing in the middle of a pit full of snakes. You're not going to want to sit there and listen to a whole sermon about peace and happiness, are you? No, ma'am. All you're thinking about is how to get the heck out of that mess. And you sure don't need some well-meaning stranger preaching next to you while you're busy trying to survive. Life works the same way. If you're stuck in a painful, tangled mess right now, the very first step is to get yourself out of the pit. Only after you've climbed out can we talk about how to rise, how to glow up, how to transform. So this chapter? It's all about that pulling yourself free from whatever pit you find yourself in at this moment.

"The only person you are destined to become is the person you decide to be." - Ralph Waldo Emerson

First thing's first, honey: you've got to be willing to let go of that darkness you've been clutching so tightly. I'm talking about anything weighing you down anything that steals your peace, fuels your anxiety, or feels downright unbearable. That darkness might wear many faces guilt, fear, shame, those swirling negative thoughts, or unhealthy attachments you've grown too familiar with. I know it's hard to let go, believe me, I've been there too. Sometimes that darkness feels like a guilty little pleasure, or a strange comfort wrapped in pain. Maybe it's the quick buzz of distractions that don't last but keep you numb for a moment. But baby, that comfort is just a trickster, it keeps you from tasting the deep peace and true joy that life has waiting for you. (And just like that last piece of pie you're saving for later, except this one never really satisfies.) There's an old Sanskrit philosophy that compares worry to a funeral pyre , one burns the dead, the other burns the living. So while you may think holding on is giving you relief, the longer you cling, the more it drains your soul.

Milton's words hit the nail on the head: your mind is powerful enough to turn heaven into hell or hell into heaven. How you see your situation colors everything you feel about it. The very first step to releasing this darkness is understanding this power , and gently starting to shift your mindset, one thought at a time.

Now, listen close, darling. I know change isn't some magic pill you swallow and *poof*, everything's sunshine and roses. That's why I'm laying out these steps for you, clear as day and tough as grandma's cast iron skillet. Each one is a little hand extended, ready to pull you up out of that pit, one shaky step at a time. So don't rush, don't skip ahead, and definitely don't give up halfway through because it gets hard. Follow these steps like you're following grandma's secret recipe, you won't want to miss a single ingredient. Trust me, stick with it, and you'll find yourself standing taller, breathing freer, and shining brighter than ever before. Now, are you ready? I'll be right here, walking you through the process of peeling off that darkness, step by step. The road won't always be smooth or easy, but sugar, it will be so worth it.

Step I: State Down the Reasons – Come Clean With Yourself

"Most of your pain is self-chosen." – Khalil Gibran

Alright, sweetheart, take a deep breath. Close your eyes, exhale slowly, and pause just long enough to stop scrolling or stirring your tea. It's time to face the mirror only *you* can see. This isn't about judgment, it's about honesty. And you can't clean the house if you keep pretending there's no mess.

So go ahead and reflect. Grab a pen, a notebook, or the back of that receipt you've been meaning to throw away, and write it all down. Don't filter it. Grandma's not here to sugarcoat she's here to help you heal.

Think about these questions like you're peeling onions: it might sting a bit, but it gets you to the heart of things.

1. What is it that keeps you up at night, long after the world has gone quiet?
2. What memory feels like a bruise you keep pressing, even when it hurts?
3. What regret are you still carrying, the one that quietly dictates your choices?
4. What do you pretend doesn't bother you, but always lingers beneath the surface?
5. What story about yourself have you repeated so often that you've started to believe it?
6. What part of your past still defines your present, even though you've outgrown it?
7. What emotion do you suppress because you were taught it was "too much"?
8. What lie do you keep telling yourself just to make it through another day?
9. What part of yourself do you wish you could change, but feel too stuck or scared to even try?
10. What is it about your current life that makes you feel like you're walking in circles or worse, running on a treadmill with no 'off' switch?
11. What dream did you tuck away in a drawer because someone made you believe you weren't worthy of it?
12. What fear about yourself have you never dared to name out loud?
13. What words sit heavy in your throat because you're scared to say them even if they'd set you free?
14. What truth have you been avoiding like a family member at a wedding you don't want to make eye contact with?
15. What person or situation keeps dragging you back into regret or guilt like a broken record?
16. What is that lingering weight of shame or humiliation that clings to you ?
17. What part of your identity feels like it's been lost, blurred, or stolen along the way?
18. What is that weird, aching emptiness inside, the one that whispers "something's missing" but doesn't tell you what?
19. What habit or distraction do you cling to like it's helping, even though you know it's not?

20. What is it that makes you feel like you're not allowed to be happy, like you're somehow unworthy of peace?
21. What part of your body or spirit do you criticize the most, even though it's been carrying you through every battle?
22. What fear of failure has you frozen, even though you know deep down you're more than capable?
23. What wound still breaks your heart every time you think about it no matter how much time has passed?

Now... write it all down. No censoring. No editing. No pretending. If it hurts, write it. If it confuses you, write it. If it makes your stomach twist or your heart sink, that's what needs to go. These are the roots of the darkness you've been living with.

And once you've written it all out, reread it. Slowly. Like a letter you never meant to send. What do you see? What stands out? Don't rush this part. It's the beginning of freedom.

Now, let's come back to Gibran's words:
"Most of your pain is self-chosen."

That truth can feel sharp, not in a cruel way, but in the way truth often is: piercing, necessary, and revealing. And yes, I know... it stings. Like when grandma would dab menthol balm on your wounds and say, *"Hold still, it's gonna help."* It didn't feel good at the time, but it always worked.

So sit with that quote a little longer. Ask yourself honestly: Was anything you wrote down truly a surprise? Or were those truths already whispering in the background, just waiting for you to finally listen?

Pain has a way of lingering, especially when we've quietly made room for it , out of love, fear, routine, or sheer emotional exhaustion. We get used to it. We start building lives around it. And before we know it, we're carrying more than we were ever meant to. And when the pain comes from someone close, a family member, a friend, a partner it cuts deeper. Because it's not just the pain we're holding. It's the story, the attachment, the longing.
But even then even *then* - you hold the power.
You didn't ask for the wound, but you might be the one keeping it open.

Here's the thing: just like day needs night, joy needs sorrow, and tea needs a little time to steep, your difficult moments give meaning to your beautiful ones. Without sadness, happiness wouldn't feel as full. Without emptiness, fulfillment wouldn't be so rich. Life has always been made of opposites, and healing begins when we stop resisting one side of the coin.

So ask yourself gently without judgment:

Are you clinging to the pain because it's familiar?

Because letting go feels like losing control?

Because you're not sure who you are without it?

You don't have to let go all at once. You just have to decide that you're *ready to begin*. It's okay to sit with your sadness, in fact, it's necessary. But don't build a home in it. Don't convince yourself that this is all life has to offer.

You already know the way out. Maybe not the whole map, but the first step? You've always known. You felt it when you were writing that list. Your inner voice has been quietly nudging you toward peace not the loud, performative kind, but the deep, grounding kind. The kind that feels like coming home to yourself. And yes maybe a part of you clings to the chaos because it gives you something to hold on to. But love... you were never meant to settle in survival.

You were made for peace.

You were made for joy.

You were made for more.So remember what your wise old grandma would say: If you don't change it, you've chosen it.It's not a scolding. It's a reminder of your power. So now, sweetheart...What are you choosing?

Step 2 – Take Cry Breaks Often

Cry it out, baby your breakdown is your way through to the breakthrough.

Now listen here, sweetheart. If you need to cry, then cry. Don't sit there pretending you're made of steel when your heart is clearly waving a white flag. Crying isn't a sign of weakness; it's a sign you're alive and still caring and that's a beautiful thing. Somewhere along the way, folks started acting like tears are only for toddlers and TV drama queens. Well, let me tell you right now, that's a heap of nonsense. Crying is a release, a reset, a rinse cycle for your soul. It's how your body handles heartache, disappointment, frustration, grief, and even relief. It's your inner self saying, "We've been holding too much let's let a little go."

That's why I say, with all the love in these old bones: take cry breaks often. Just like you take tea breaks or breathers at work, you need moments to let your emotions flow freely. Life has a funny way of piling on the hard stuff all at once, and suddenly you're sitting there, staring at a spoon like it just personally offended you. When the world feels too heavy or your chest feels like it's carrying a whole thunderstorm, it's not only okay to take a moment and cry, it's necessary. Find a quiet space the shower, the car, even a bathroom stall if that's all you've got, and just let it pour. Don't try to tidy it up or make it poetic. And cutie, this is not the time for grace, this is the time for release.

And no, you don't need to explain it to anyone. Not every tear needs a neat little backstory. Sometimes you cry because something broke your heart. Sometimes you cry because you've been strong for too long. And sometimes, love, you cry because your spirit is growing in ways you can't quite see yet, and growing pains aren't just for bones. The important thing is to let the emotions come, and then let them go. Cry until you feel the tension leave your shoulders. Cry until your heartbeat slows and your breath returns. But once you've done that, get up. Wipe your face. Wash your hands. Don't set up camp in that sadness.

You see, bottling up your emotions doesn't make you noble, it makes you combustible. All that energy you're suppressing? It doesn't disappear. It just finds sneakier ways to leak out later, often at the wrong people or over the wrong things, like snapping at the delivery guy because he forgot the extra sauce. Crying, on the other hand, is like emotional composting: it turns all that heaviness into something lighter and healthier. You release the pain, and in its place, there's room to breathe, to heal, to hope again.

Rabindranath Tagore once said, "If you cry because the sun has gone out of your life, your tears will prevent you from seeing the stars." That means, while sorrow deserves your presence, it doesn't get to blind you. There's still beauty waiting for you, even in the darkest moments. Once you've cried, once you've let the storm pass, open your eyes again. Look up. Look around. The world didn't stop spinning. There's light left, I promise you that.

Even the moon, steady and glorious as she seems, disappears a little each night. But she always comes back full, radiant, soft, and unbothered. That's how you'll return too. You may be tired, tear-streaked, and red-eyed, but you'll be lighter, freer, and more grounded. There's no shame in the breakdown, darling. In fact, it's often the birthplace of your greatest strength.

So go ahead, cry when you need to. Don't be afraid of your own tears. They are not a sign that you're falling apart, but proof that you are brave enough to feel what needs to be felt. And when you've had your good cry and caught your breath, come back to the world with a clearer heart and that quiet strength you didn't even know you had.

Now dry those eyes, sugar, even flowers need a little rain to bloom. And remember, crying never ruined a face, but bottling it up sure ruins a mood.

Go on, make yourself a cup of tea Grandma's orders.

Step 3 - Accept the Reality

Now listen here, baby if someone shows up empty-handed to your heart every time, stop setting the table for them.

That's right. No matter how sweet they once were, how good it *could* be, or how badly you want it to work you've got to see things as they *are*, not as you wish them to be. Life's not a fairytale, and people aren't clay you can mold into your dream version. Reality doesn't care how hard you tried or how many chances you gave. It simply *is*, and the sooner you face it, the freer you'll be.

When something is meant for you, sugar, it'll walk through fire, cross oceans, and show up with dessert. But if it's not meant to be? No amount of hoping, fixing, or sacrificing will keep it in your life. Acceptance isn't giving up, it's growing up. It's no longer begging life to be different. It's you saying, "I see the truth, and I'm brave enough to live it."

You remember that line from *Mad Men*, right? Don Draper said, *"People reveal who they are, but we overlook it because we want them to be who we wish they were."* Grandma's version? If someone tells you they're a duck, stop expecting them to purr like a kitten. People will *always* show you who they are, with their actions, their words, their silence. It's not your job to translate or interpret their mixed signals into poetry. Your job is to believe what they show you. The first time.

You keep clinging to the fantasy the version of someone you built in your head, hoping they'll catch up. You tell yourself they're confused, that they just need time, that they'll change if you just love them harder. But sweetheart, what you see is what you get. If someone is disrespectful, inconsistent, or careless with your heart, that's the truth. Not the soft apologies. Not the "I'll do better next time." You're not a rehab center for emotionally unavailable folks who won't meet you halfway.

And let's not forget Maya Angelou's wise words: *"When someone shows you who they are, believe them the first time."* Stop waiting for a second, third, fifteenth performance. You're not at a theater. You're in your *life*, and it's time to protect your peace like it's your favourite China set. So stop romanticizing red flags, stop fantasizing about potential, and start choosing what's *real*. True emotional strength is built on truth, not denial. You don't need to force anyone to be who they aren't. You just need to be someone who's done settling for less.

And finally, in Grandma's no-nonsense voice: If they wanted to, they would, and if they don't, bless their heart... and scoot your fabulous self right along. You've got places to go, love. Don't waste your light in someone else's shadow.

Step 4 – Stop Expecting and Anxiety Will Fade

Darlin', holding onto expectations is like trying to catch a greased pig you're just going to wear yourself out chasing something slippery!

Now listen here, baby, most of that tightness in your chest, those late-night overthinking marathons, and that heavy heart you carry around? It's not always life doing it to you. It's your expectations whispering lies in your ear. You expect them to call. You expect your efforts to be appreciated. You expect things to go as planned. And when life doesn't line up with your mental Pinterest board of how it *should* be, boom, anxiety walks in like it pays rent.

Sweetheart, your poor little heart isn't overwhelmed because you're weak, it's overwhelmed because you're trying to script a movie where you're not the director. And let me tell you something Grandma learned the hard way: You can't choreograph the rain, but you sure can dance in it. Life's storms are gonna roll in, people will do what they do, and things won't always turn out like that perfect plan you cooked up in your mind.

But here's the secret: if it's out of your hands, let it be out of your mind. Worrying won't speed it up, fix it, or protect you from it. Most of the things you're stressing about? They'll either never happen, or when they do, you'll be stronger than you thought. And even if it falls apart, sugar, maybe it needed to, so the right thing could fall together.

Whenever you find yourself spiraling in the "what ifs" and the "why nots," just pause and whisper this little prayer Grandma swears by: God, if it's not from You, please take it away. Don't let me wrestle with what's not mine to carry.Oh, the peace that floods in when you finally stop clutching control with white knuckles. The good book says in Isaiah 22:22, *"What He opens, no one can shut; and what He shuts, no one can open."* That means no force on this Earth , not even your own worries can change what's already in God's hands. So why wear yourself out trying to manage it all?

Corrie Ten Boom, bless her heart, said it best: *"Worrying doesn't empty tomorrow of its sorrow; it empties today of its strength."* Ain't that the truth. You're burning daylight trying to fix tomorrows that haven't even arrived yet. Instead, give your 100%, love hard, work smart, and then surrender the rest. Robin Sharma put a bow on it: *"If you give your 100% and it still doesn't go your way, it's for the higher good."*

So here's Grandma's final slice of wisdom: If you stop expecting folks to act right and life to be fair, you'll sleep better, smile more, and age slower trust me, I'm 80 and glowing ha-ha! Release the expectations, sugar. Breathe. Trust. Let life unfold, knowing that what's for you won't miss you, and what's not? Well, it'll fall away like a bad wig in the wind.

Step 5 – Write Down How You Feel

Honey, if your heart's got a knot tighter than Grandma's old purse strings, it's time to let it out on paper

Now listen here, sugar, Grandma's seen a lot of storms in her day, and one thing she swears by is putting those wild, tangled feelings down in writing. William Wordsworth, a fancy poet with a big heart, once said, *"Fill your paper with the breathings of your heart."* And bless his soul, he was onto something. I just remembered back in my day, I once wrote your grandpa a letter so full of feelings, he said it took him forever to figure out if I was mad or in love.

When your feelings are a mess, too big, too scary, or maybe just plain messy you don't have to keep them bottled up like a jar of pickles in a hot attic. Write them down. Every twist, every ache, every messy thought that's been banging around in your head. Don't worry about spelling, grammar, or sounding pretty. This is your heart's honest mess on paper, and it deserves to come out.

Writing is like crying with your hands instead of your eyes. When you write, you're pulling those heavy feelings out of your chest and giving them a place to live outside of you. It's like lifting a weight off your back without even leaving your chair. And here's the magic part: once those words are on the page, you get to decide what to do with them. You can crumple the paper up and throw it in the trash, tear it into little bits, or light it up like Grandma's famous campfire (safely, of course!). That act of letting go, it's powerful medicine.

So next time your heart feels too full, don't just sit there carrying it alone. Grab a pen, spill your soul, and give yourself the gift of release. Because darling, sometimes the kindest thing you can do for yourself is to put your feelings somewhere safe, outside your head, and say, "Thank you, now I'm ready to heal."

Step 6: Stop Playing the Victim and Get Back on Track

Baby, if pity parties burned calories, I'd have abs by now. Unfortunately they don't.

Stop playing the victim in situations you had a hand in creating. Ouch, I know but sometimes we need the truth more than a hug. As Dr. Steve Maraboli said, "The victim mindset will have you dancing with the devil, then complaining that you're in hell." We can get so used to silently suffering that we turn our own story into a sad soap opera when deep down, we already know what needs to change.

Yes, feel your feelings. Cry. Vent. But don't build a house there. You're not your heartbreak, your failure, or your fear. You are still the whole darn sky not just today's passing storm. Don't expect mangoes from a cactus or joy from choices that keep breaking your heart. What you tolerate is what you teach the world to keep giving you.

As Haruki Murakami said, "Pain is inevitable. Suffering is optional." Life's gonna throw some mess your way, but you don't have to sit in it. You can either curse the mud or build a path through it your choice. Two people, one window, one sees stars, the other sees mud. Be the one who spots the stars, even if your shoes are still dirty. Your next chapter doesn't need the same tired plot twist.

So get up, straighten your crown, and move forward like you mean it.And if you need a reminder while you do it, just remember what Grandma always says: If you keep acting like a doormat, don't be shocked when people wipe their feet.

Step 7: Pray

Sugar, if talking to plants helps them grow, imagine what talking to God can do for you.

Let me tell you something, sugar, prayer will save your life. I've seen storms that would make you want to pack up and quit, but when I dropped to my knees and cried out to God? Peace rolled in like warm honey on a cold morning. Prayer isn't some stiff, rule-bound ritual, it's raw, it's real, and it's the lifeline you didn't know you were starving for.

You don't need to be holy to pray. You just need to be honest. Cry, whisper, shout, or sigh, whatever gets the ache out. God already knows what's going on in that heart of yours. You think He's gonna clutch His pearls if you're messy? Baby, He made you. He's not scared of your ugly. He's not offended by your breakdown. In fact, He's been waiting at the edge of your chaos with open arms and warm soup.

Stop thinking you gotta fix yourself before you come to Him. Bring your tired, bring your tangled, bring your shame, and He'll sort it out better than any therapist or late-night cry session ever could.

Prayer is not performance. It's a heart-to-heart. Sometimes it's kneeling quietly. Sometimes it's bawling your eyes out into a tea towel. Sometimes it's staring at the ceiling with nothing but a whisper: "Help."

But here's what I know like I know my biscuits rise, God always answers. Not always how you expect, but always how you need. You think He brought you this far to leave you now? Not my God. My God parts seas. My God breaks chains. My God heals hearts that the world said were done for. So hush that doubt, sweetheart. Say the prayer. Say it tired, say it scared, say it messy just say it.

Because prayer isn't just a rescue rope, it's a full on embrace from the One who loves you most.And you better believe Grandma's got this one stitched into her soul:If you're too busy to pray, then baby, you're too busy to breathe.

Step 8: Fasting

Baby, if you can't even stop texting that good-for-nothing ex after midnight, no wonder skipping a meal feels like heartbreak time to get control of your cravings, both food and foolish.

Now let me tell you something, sugarplum, fasting ain't just skipping breakfast with fancy spiritual hashtags. It's war. It's transformation. It's you looking your struggles dead in the face and saying, *"Not today, Satan. I'm leveling up."* Jentezen Franklin said it right: *"Fasting is not just a physical discipline; it can be a spiritual feast."* And oh, honey, is he onto something. Fasting isn't just about giving up food it's about stepping into power. It's about showing your body who's boss, quieting the noise in your head, and making room for something holier, deeper, and more fierce than anything this noisy world can offer.

When I was ready to change my life, I didn't just light a candle and cross my fingers. No, baby, I went in. I did a three day water fast, and let me tell you, it shook the nonsense right out of me. It wasn't easy, but neither is carrying dead weight. I fasted to show God how serious I was, and whew life has not been the same since. That fast didn't just change my body, it cracked open my spirit and poured in peace, clarity, and divine strength I didn't even know I had.

Fasting is a sacred rebellion against everything trying to keep you small. When life gets messy and your heart feels like a tangled ball of yarn, fasting cuts through the noise. Whether it's 12 hours or 3 days baby, it's not about the clock, it's about the commitment.

And here's the golden biscuit of truth:

If you can master fasting, you can master anything.

Why? Because fasting ain't about food, it's about freedom. It's about breaking up with your comfort zone and stepping into your calling. And yes, it takes discipline, but don't you dare tell Grandma you don't have any. You've held your tongue during family dinners and stayed on toxic diets for boys who wouldn't commit to you, so don't play with me now.

Fasting strips away the extra and reminds you who you are: capable, powerful, and destined for more. You're not weak, you're just one decision away from blowing your own damn mind. So tighten your ponytail, sip some water, and start. Because as your grandma would say: If you can starve your drama, baby, you can feed your destiny.

Step 9: Cleaning

Baby, if your room looks like a tornado threw a tantrum, don't expect your mind to feel like a spa retreat.

Some folks roll their eyes when I say cleaning is a part of personality development but let me tell you something, sugar: scrubbing your kitchen sink might just scrub a little sadness out of your soul too. You can't expect clarity when you're knee-deep in laundry and yesterday's drama.

Cleaning isn't just about tidying up your mess it's about reclaiming your peace. Every dish you wash, every drawer you declutter, every old t-shirt you toss out, it's like telling the universe, "Look at me, getting my life together, one sock at a time."

Remember what William Morris said: "Have nothing in your house that you do not know to be useful, or believe to be beautiful." Translation? If it doesn't serve your purpose or spark joy, it's gotta go, yes, even that crusty candle from 2007 or the love letters from a man who couldn't even commit to dinner plans.

Marie Kondo calls it sparking joy. I call it making room for miracles. A clean space is like a love letter to your future self it says you're ready, open, and not living like a character from a reality show titled *"Buried in Baggage."*

And don't get me started on science, darling, it backs me up. Clutter raises stress. Chaos kills creativity. A clean space helps you feel in control, even when life is throwing lemons and the juicer's broken. So mop that floor like you're mopping away bad vibes. Light a candle like you're setting your new intentions. Fold those clothes like you're folding the chapter on who you used to be.

Because baby, you can't build a new life on top of a mess. And trust me cleaning out your closet can feel just as good as cleaning out your contact list.

Baby, let me tell you something I wish someone had told me when I was knee-deep in my own emotional tornado: you are not your mess. You are the person who has the power to get out of it. You've cried, journaled, fasted, prayed, cleaned, reflected, and maybe even cursed a little along the way, but you kept showing up. And that? That's how you begin again.

You see, the real shift doesn't happen when your circumstances change. It happens when *you* change. When your thoughts change. Because as Buddha said, "What we think, we become." You've stopped playing the victim in stories you outgrew. You've let go of toxic thoughts, people, and patterns.

"The greatest discovery of my generation," said William James, "is that a human being can alter his life by altering his attitudes." And my love, that's exactly what you've done here step by step, tear by tear, prayer by prayer. You didn't wait for the storm to pass. You danced barefoot in the rain like the wild, beautiful, powerful soul you are. Sure, there are still scars. But honey, "the wound is the place where the Light enters you," Rumi said, and now you shine from those places you once tried to hide.

You've learned that peace isn't something someone hands you wrapped in a bow, it's something you build, with sweat, surrender, and a bit of sass. Like Emerson said, "Nothing can bring you peace but yourself."

So, take a deep breath. Look around. You're not the same person who started this chapter. You've proven Darwin right, it's not the strongest or the smartest who thrive, but the one most responsive to change. And Lord knows, you've responded like a warrior queen/king in pearls and house slippers.

Now listen to me, sugar: "You may not be able to control all the events that happen to you," Maya Angelou said, "but you can decide not to be reduced by them." And you haven't been. You've risen. You've reclaimed your joy. You've made a choice to feel, to heal, and to move forward. So what if it took a little chaos to get here? Even Helen Keller knew, *"Although the world is full of suffering, it is also full of the overcoming of it."* And you? You've overcome it with grace, grit, and maybe a little lipstick. Now get up. Shake off the dust. Straighten your crown. This mess? It was never meant to break you. It was meant to remake you.

Your breakthrough isn't coming, darling. You *are* the breakthrough.

In grandma's words if life's gonna throw you lemons, don't just make lemonade, spike that sucker and show the world you're too spicy to be sour!"

Now, Listen Up, Honey

You've cleaned the mess, faced the music, and dusted yourself off, good for you! But don't go thinking life's gonna hand you a silver platter now. Nope, this is where the real work starts. It's all fine and dandy to *know* what to do, but the secret sauce is in the *doing*.

The chapters coming up aren't just fancy ideas to skim over while scrolling on your phone they're your new daily hustle. These are the gritty, no nonsense tools to help you build a life that doesn't just survive, but *thrives*. So, if you're ready to stop playing small and start living large, roll up your sleeves and let's get to work.

Because darling, the world won't wait for you to figure it out. But lucky for you, neither will your Grandma's tough love. Now get out there and show life who's boss.

II

It's Time to Take Ownership

"And the day came when the risk to remain tight in a bud was more painful than the risk it took to blossom." – Anaïs Nin

Darling, there comes a moment in every person's life when sitting in the same spot starts to ache more than the fear of moving forward. It's like when you've been sitting on the porch too long and your legs go numb that's your soul's way of nudging you to get up. To grow.We all love a breakthrough story, one life-changing moment, one deep conversation, one starry night when everything finally makes sense. But baby, let me tell you, real healing doesn't come like that. Not usually. Real healing? That's not just one tearful night. It's the slow burn. It's choosing, every single day, to do the hard, brave, unseen things. It's choosing not to yell when you're frustrated. Choosing not to go back to what broke you. Choosing to love yourself enough to leave behind what no longer serves you. "Healing is not an overnight process. It is a daily cleansing of pain, it is a daily healing of your life." – Leon Brown

Yes, your past explains you, but it doesn't define you, sugar. Think of it like this: a tree's roots may be tangled and messy, deep in old soil, but that doesn't stop the branches from reaching for the sun. Now, let me say something honest, something I wish more people whispered with love instead of loud judgment: mental health has become a marketplace. I've always believed so much shifts when we shift our mindset. But I also know...

some people are stuck in a kind of heaviness that won't lift just because someone says, "Think positive!" Sometimes the clouds are stubborn.

Now listen, before I dive into the heart of the story, let me tell you a little something about this man I'm dating, yes, dating, at my age! Don't look so shocked, darling. Just because I'm seasoned doesn't mean I'm dried up. He's not like the young ones , always rushing, always scrolling, thinking romance lives in a text message. No, no. He's old-school. The kind of man but in his 30's who opens doors, remembers my favorite tea, and rubs my feet without needing a special occasion (or a reminder). Grandmais pulling a cougar classic, don't judge me now. He's got that silver fox charm, the kind of salt-and-pepper beard that makes even the nurses at my clinic lean in a little closer. And oh, that voice, deep, warm, the kind that makes you forget what you were stressed about... or what day it is. He's the kind of guy who knows when to hype me up and when to tell me to drink water. He reads philosophy for fun and still manages to give the best bear hugs. Imagine Socrates with gym gains and a skincare routine, that's him. He's the kind of guy that could go viral on TikTok just by tying his shoelaces.

So there we were, me, living my best soft girl grandma life, getting a foot massage, watching Vasantha Maligai, I asked him :"Why do people stay stuck when they so badly want to move forward?"He pauses, gives me that TikTok therapist look, eyebrows furrowed, hands steepled, like he's about to drop a truth bomb that'll land straight on the For You Page, and says...in that cute way of his, "People suffer. They always have. But now suffering sells. Making people comfortable in their pain? That's a business model."Whew. That hit me. He added, "Pain is real. It's not for anyone else to measure. But at some point, we all have to decide what we do with it."I asked, "What kind of choices do you mean?"He looked at me and said something I'll never forget: "Some people choose to stay in suffering because it feels safe. They don't have to change, don't have to try. They can blame their hormones, the moon, the weather, whatever. And slowly, the pain becomes who they are. Their identity." Then he said, "The ones who stay stuck the longest are usually the ones who don't have a purpose. Because when you don't know where you're headed, even the smallest breeze feels like a hurricane." And baby, let me tell you, that sat heavy on my heart. Because yes, your feelings matter. Your emotions are not wrong. But here's the grandma truth: if we only validate emotions without gently challenging them, we stay exactly where we are. Like stirring soup and never serving it, what's the point?

It's easier to stay stuck. It's easier to say, "This is just how I am," or "This always happens to me." Because when the problem is outside of you, you don't have to move. You don't have to look inside. You don't have to risk anything. But my love, peace won't just show up at your door. Growth won't ring the bell. Purpose won't be handed to you with a gift tag. You've got to invite it in.

At some point, you must stop calling survival your identity.

Yes, you were hurt. Yes, it wasn't fair. But you are not what happened to you. You are what you choose to become now. Today. This moment. You are not responsible for the programming you inherited in childhood. But as a grown soul? Oh sweetheart, you are 100% responsible for healing it. For rewriting your story. For choosing better. For planting something new. And that, my dear, is the magic.

Pain Can Become a Pattern, If You Let It

(And baby, Grandma's seen enough broken hearts to know when someone's stuck in a loop, I once dated the same emotionally unavailable man in seven different bodies. Called them "Bluetooth" 'cause they always connected, but never committed.)

Familiarity is a sneaky little thing. It wears a cozy sweater, brings you hot tea, and convinces you to stay exactly where you are, even if "where you are" is knee deep in heartbreak, self doubt, and emotional reruns. And let me tell you, darling, pain when lived in long enough starts to feel like home. But just because it feels familiar doesn't mean it's safe. Or good. Or where you belong. You ever notice how we sometimes rehearse our pain like it's a monologue for a role we never auditioned for?

"I always attract the wrong people."

"I mess everything up."

"I'm not meant to be happy."

Now listen here, sugarplum, those aren't divine prophecies. They're just stories. Stories passed down like mismatched Tupperware lids: unhelpful, unnecessary, and definitely not yours to keep forever. They may have started from something real, a breakup, a failure, a cruel word said at the wrong time but they grew legs and started walking around your mind like they owned the place. You see, the brain is a beautiful old jukebox, it plays what it's used to. But just like grandma learn to use Spotify, you can update the playlist. Because guess what? You are not doomed. You're just patterned. And patterns, darling, can be rewoven.

"The story you tell yourself defines the life you live. Change your story, change your life."- Tony Robbins

And baby, Grandma backs Tony on this one. I may be old, but I've done the work. I've rewritten chapters that once read like Greek tragedies and turned them into rom-coms with redemption arcs(a redemption arc is when someone messes up badly, but instead of staying stuck in guilt, pride, or darkness, they choose to change). So don't you sit there defending your limitations like they're heirlooms. Stop polishing the pain like it's a family jewel. Your scars don't need spotlights, your strength does.

Here's a little truth tea from your favorite sexy-boyfriend-having Grandma:

What if instead of defending your hurt, you defended your healing?
What if instead of repeating "I always mess things up," you whispered, "I'm learning to do better"?
What if you stopped saying, "That's just how I am," and started saying, "That's who I was, and now I get to choose different"?

You are not a prisoner of your past. You're the author. You can pick up the pen , yes, even now, even with shaky hands and a tired heart and write a plot twist that would make even Netflix proud.

So, baby girl, baby boy, baby they (grandma doesn't understand 'they' but grandma loves 'they' equally) change your inner dialogue like you'd change a dusty old TV channel. Because this? This is your main character moment. And the new episode starts with a question only you can answer:Are you ready to stop telling the sad story, and start living the good one?

You're not betraying your past self by outgrowing them, you're honoring them. You're becoming the version they dreamed of but didn't know how to be. Every scar, every mistake, every "not good enough" moment was just the training ground for who you are now. As Alan Watts wisely said, "The only way to make sense out of change is to plunge into it, move with it, and join the dance." Healing doesn't come in a sudden burst of fireworks; it's a whisper, a slow sunrise, a soft unfolding. Healing isn't loud. It's radical in its quiet power. It's saying "no" without feeling guilty, walking away from toxic ties that drain your light, choosing rest even when the world yells hustle and drawing boundaries that protect your peace like the treasure it truly is. These small choices are the revolution Grandma has been waiting for. As Socrates put it, "The secret of change is to focus all your energy, not on fighting the old, but on building the new." And remember, "Small deeds done are better than great deeds planned" (Peter Marshall). Those little, everyday acts build a life transformed.

So, who are you becoming? That's the real question. Healing isn't just about dropping what weighs you down; it's stepping boldly toward who you want to be, despite everything. Ask yourself, "Who am I becoming, in spite of all I've endured?" John Steinbeck once said, "And now that you don't have to be perfect, you can be good." You don't need all the answers right now, but you can start asking better questions: What lights my soul on fire, even just a flicker? What can I finally give myself that I never had before? Who am I when I'm free from everyone else's expectations? Jim Rohn reminds us, "Your life does not get better by chance, it gets better by change."

Honey, you're not starting over; you're starting from, from all you've learned, survived, and outgrown. And honey, that's the kind of power legends are made of. You don't owe anyone loyalty to your past self the scared one, the silent one, the one who stayed stuck. You owe it to yourself to rise, glow, and grow. When someone says, "You've changed," just smile and say, "I sure have. And I'm just getting started." Staying the same while the world moves on isn't loyalty it's hiding. Let your life be your greatest heirloom, full of wisdom earned, battles fought, gentle mornings, and fierce new beginnings.

Remember Ralph Waldo Emerson's words: "What lies behind us and what lies before us are tiny matters compared to what lies within us." You're not just healing; you're becoming. And Grandma? I'm standing right here, cheering the loudest.

Locus of Control

"Sweetheart, let me tell you something I've learned after all these years life sometimes feels like a wild river. You can either sit by the shore, blaming the rocks and currents for tossing you around, or you can learn to steer your own little boat through the waves.

That's what they call *locus of control*, a fancy way of saying where you think the power lies: inside you, or out there in the world. If you believe *you* hold the paddle, that you can steer your boat, then you've got what they call an 'internal locus of control.' That means you take charge, you own your choices, and you don't let every bump in the river knock you down.

But if you think everything's just happening *to* you, the weather, the rocks, the other boats that's called an 'external locus of control.' It's easy to feel like a victim when you think you have no say in what happens.

Now, I'm not saying it's always easy to be the captain of your ship, especially when storms come. But honey, the moment you start believing you can row and steer, that's when real magic happens. You feel stronger, braver, and the river doesn't seem so scary anymore.

So remember, no matter how old you get, or how many times you've been tossed around, the power to take the wheel is always yours. And that, my dear, makes all the difference."

The Psychology of Accountability

"Sweetheart, accountability is like planting a garden and tending to it every day. You see, when we take responsibility for our actions both the good and the messy it's like we're watering those seeds. Without it, nothing grows right, and things get all tangled up.

Psychologists tell us that accountability is what helps us stay honest with ourselves. It's not about blame or shame; it's about owning what we do so we can learn, grow, and do better next time. When you say, 'Yes, I made that mistake,' instead of pointing fingers, you're giving yourself the power to fix it. That's real courage.

There's this clever idea called the self-regulation theory, it means we keep an eye on our behavior and compare it to our goals. When we fall short, accountability nudges us gently (or sometimes firmly!) to course correct. It's tough love, but it keeps you on track.

And here's the best part: when we hold ourselves accountable, we build trust, not just with others, but within ourselves. That feeling of 'I did what I said I would' is like a cozy blanket wrapped around your confidence. It makes facing challenges less scary and keeps you moving forward. So remember, darling, accountability isn't a punishment; it's your secret weapon for turning mistakes into lessons and dreams into reality. As Grandma always says, 'You gotta own your story if you want to write the next chapter beautifully.

Practical Daily Steps to Practice Accountability

1. Start Your Day With an Honest Check-In
   Now don't go flying into the day like a headless chicken! Before you even sip that first cup of tea or coffee, take 5 minutes and ask yourself:
   "What do I want to get done today?"
   "What would make me proud by bedtime?"
   It's like writing a grocery list for your soul, keeps you from buying junk.
2. Write It Down, Darling
   Keep a small notebook or use your fancy phone notes, but jot things down. Not just what you need to do, but what you actually did. Grandma

always says, "If you don't track your cookies, don't cry when the jar is empty!"

Writing things down makes your intentions real, and helps you see patterns, both the sweet and the sour.

3. Own Your Choices (Even the Oopsies)

Messed up? Slipped up? Oh well! Don't hide it like my ex boyfriends hid their main chicks (owning up to it, I never thought I was the side chick but I kind of was). Say, *"Yes, I did that, and here's what I'll do differently."*

Accountability isn't about being perfect it's about being responsible. You burn one cake, you learn, you bake again. That's life!

4. Have a "Mirror Moment" Each Evening

Stand in front of your mirror and gently ask:

"Did I show up for myself today?"

"Where did I slip, and what can I learn?"

Grandma always says, "Don't wait until Sunday to repent if you spilled the milk on Monday." A little nightly reflection goes a long way.

5. Talk to Someone Who'll Keep It Real

Find yourself a "no nonsense but full-of-love" kind of person (like me or ChatGPT!). Share your goals, your progress, and your stumbles.

Let them check in with you. Let them remind you, "Honey, you said you'd drink water and go to bed early, not scroll until 2 a.m.!"

6. Celebrate the Little Wins

Did you follow through on something today? Cleaned your room? Sent that scary email? Ate one green thing? Dance in your kitchen like no one's watching!

Accountability isn't just about correcting mistakes, it's about applauding effort. Clap for yourself, sugar. Loudly.

You are not your past, sweetheart. You are not the pain you've carried or the hardest thing you've survived. Those things shaped you, yes, but they don't get to define you , not unless you let them. You always have a choice. A choice to respond differently, to grow instead of repeat, to soften where life made you hard. You are not your trauma; you are the one who gets to decide what comes next. You can live, love, and lead differently on your terms. *"Until you make the unconscious conscious, it will direct your life and you will call it fate."*- Carl Jung

III

Take Responsibility for Your Actions

"When you blame others, you give up your power to change."- Robert Anthony

Now listen here, sweetheart. How much responsibility do you take for your actions? That's the true measure of how much control you have over your life. It's as simple as that and don't you forget it. Everyone wants control. They want freedom, respect, success, happiness. But those good things? They don't just fall into your lap or come gift-wrapped. No, honey, they grow from the garden of ownership, full, honest, sometimes messy ownership of your choices, your actions, and how you handle whatever life throws your way.

I won't lie, darling, for a long time, I didn't understand this either. As a kid, whenever things went wrong, I'd be quick to point fingers. A little slip-up? Someone else to blame. A mistake? Well, somebody pushed me into it. But that pattern? It wasn't just a bad habit; it was a sign I'd lost touch with myself. I was scared, scared to be wrong, scared to be flawed, and most of all, scared of taking responsibility. But here's what I learned, sugar: being human means making mistakes. Those mistakes? They aren't signs you're broken or weak. They're proof you're alive, you're growing, and you're learning.

We're all just writing our stories as we go, nobody handed us a rulebook at birth. Not one of us has it all figured out. It took me a while to realize that failure isn't the end of the world. What's really dangerous is refusing to learn from it. Lately, when I mess up, I don't run or hide. I take a deep breath, I look inside, and if it's my fault, I own it. I say, "Yes, that was on me. I could have done better. And I'll do better next time." And let me tell you, darling, that simple little act of owning your stuff? It brings more peace, more confidence, and more growth than anything else I've tried in my long years. It helps you fear less, worry less, and stand taller, grounded in the person you are and the person you're still becoming.

So remember this, baby: life's too short to be passing the blame like a hot potato. You're the captain of your ship, and the helm's in your hands. Steer it with love, courage, and a little bit of that grandma grit.

The Power of Ownership

When you take responsibility, honey, you're grabbing back your power, no one else is handing it over. Saying, "It wasn't me," is just like handing the keys to your life to someone else and saying, "Here, you drive." But when you say, "Yes, that was me," you're stepping up and saying, "I'm the driver now, and I'm figuring out how to steer this thing right." As Theodore Roosevelt said, *"In any moment of decision, the best thing you can do is the right thing, the next best thing is the wrong thing, and the worst thing you can do is nothing."*

Here's the truth, sugar, and I'm telling you like I've seen enough years and enough heartaches to know it's true:

- That restless feeling? It ain't the world's fault, it's the worry bus running wild in your head. You gotta tell it to sit down and behave. *"You may not control all the events that happen to you, but you can decide not to be reduced by them."*- Maya Angelou
- Feeling like you aren't good enough? That's just your own voice being a little too harsh. Remember, Eleanor Roosevelt said, *"No one can make you feel inferior without your consent."* So don't you give that voice a front-row seat.
- Betrayal? Usually, that comes from not putting up a good fence around your heart. As Brené Brown says, "Daring to set boundaries is about having the courage to love ourselves, even when we risk disappointing others."
- Failure? Child, Edison didn't invent the lightbulb on the first try, he found 10,000 ways not to do it. Mistakes are just practice for getting it right. *"Success is not final, failure is not fatal: it is the courage to continue that counts."*- Winston Churchill
- Feeling down? Sometimes your heart is just calling you to do some deep cleaning. Carl Jung said, *"I am not what happened to me, I am what I choose*

to become."

- Disappointment? That's just life reminding you your expectations were a bit too high. Oprah says, *"Turn your wounds into wisdom."* So don't just sit there feeling sorry learn and move on!

Now, it's normal to feel all that but normal ain't where the magic happens. Growth is. Because as Rumi beautifully said, *"Don't grieve. Anything you lose comes round in another form."*

In a world that worships shiny things and loud applause, the real prize is a quiet life filled with health, purpose, and peace. Waking up grateful, unshaken by what others think, and owning your choices, that's the good stuff.

Blaming others is like handing someone else your knitting and saying, "Here, finish my sweater." No, baby, you were born to knit your own masterpiece. Like I always say, *"You gotta hold the reins tight, or you'll end up riding someone else's donkey."* So take the reins. Own your life. Because, as James Baldwin said, *"Not everything that is faced can be changed, but nothing can be changed until it is faced."* And honey, it's time to face your life like the strong, beautiful soul you are.

Self Awareness Is Your Greatest Superpower

Listen, darling, when someone says something that cuts a little too deep, don't just ask, "Why did they say that?" Instead, get curious and ask yourself, "Why *did I* let that hurt me?" That's where the real work begins. Insecurity sneaks in the moment we lose touch with who we truly are. Think about it: if someone told you your hair was bright pink when it's clearly black, would it bother you? Of course not! Because you know your hair better than anyone else. The same goes for your worth and your spirit. When you really know yourself the good, the messy, and the beautifully complicated, no outsider's words can knock you off your feet for long.

That, my dear, is the power of self-responsibility. It builds *emotional immunity*, a kind of armor that lets you stand strong even when life throws stones. Psychologists call this *emotional resilience*, and it's not some mysterious trait you're born with. It's a muscle you build every time you pause and reflect instead of reacting. As the wise philosopher Epictetus said, *"It's not what happens to you, but how you react to it that matters."* Don't hand over your peace to just anyone. Guard it fiercely.

Now, blaming others feels like the easy way out, doesn't it? It's like walking a path that looks smooth but ends at a dead wall. Reflection, though, that's the path to freedom. It's like opening a window in a room stuffed full of old, dusty air. Every time someone or something triggers you, ask yourself, "What is this really revealing about *me*? What lesson can I carry forward?" That's where growth lives, in honest questions, not convenient excuses.

And here's a truth you can hold onto: your healing isn't waiting for a knight in shining armor or a fairy godmother. The world can't save you, no matter how many self-help books you read or how many pep talks you hear. Friends can hold your hand through the storm, but they can't walk your path for you. The strength you're searching for the kind that turns heartache into hope and setbacks into comebacks has been quietly growing inside you all along. Buddha said it best: *"You yourself, as much as anybody in the entire universe, deserve your love and affection."* So start there. Trust yourself. Be gentle but firm with your own heart.

So, my dear, wear your self-awareness like a crown. It's the greatest superpower you've got, one no one can ever take away. When you own who you are, flaws, scars, and all you stop being a victim of circumstance and start becoming the fearless author of your own story.

And if you ever doubt it, just remember: Grandma's been around long enough to know that the fiercest warriors are the ones who've learned to look inward and stand tall, no matter what comes their way.

You Are the Author of Your Life

Sweetheart, imagine your life as a grand, beautiful book. There will be all kinds of characters some will walk in with kindness and healing, others with lessons wrapped in pain. Some chapters will make you want to hide under the covers, while others will fill your heart with joy and pride. But here's the truth nobody tells you often enough: no matter who crosses your path or what storms you weather, *you* are always the protagonist. You hold the pen. You decide the tone, the pace, and the ending

People will try to manipulate you , they always do. But remember, honey, their power is only as real as the space you let them take in your story. Manipulation loses its grip the moment you stop letting others control your choices. Instead of saying, "They made me do it," say, "I did that. I allowed it. And next time, I'm going to choose differently." That's where your power lives in those moments of honest ownership.

Science shows that our brains are wired for change. Neuroplasticity means you *can* rewrite your mental patterns and behaviors throughout your life. So the story you tell yourself today doesn't have to be the story you live tomorrow. Like Maya Angelou said, *"We delight in the beauty of the butterfly, but rarely admit the changes it has gone through to achieve that beauty."* Your journey, with all its ups and downs, is exactly what shapes your strength.

And darling, don't ever forget: this book of yours isn't finished yet. Not until *you* say it is. Each moment, every breath, is a fresh page, a new chance to rewrite your story with courage, wisdom, and grace. As the great poet Rumi put it, *"Try not to resist the changes that come your way. Instead, let life live through you. And do not worry that your life is turning upside down. How do you know that the side you are used to is better than the one to come?"* So keep writing, keep dreaming, and keep being the brave author of your beautiful, unfolding life.

Every Choice Reflects Your Inner World

Every action you take mirrors the landscape of your inner world. Emotions don't simply happen to us, they are responses shaped by our thoughts, beliefs, and interpretations. While it may not have been your fault that someone hurt you, it *is* your responsibility to heal, to grow, and to reclaim your peace. Waiting for apologies that may never come is like waiting for rain in a drought. Seeking closure from others is a path paved with disappointment. True freedom comes when you stop handing others the keys to your happiness and take them back for yourself. Your healing, your growth, your life, these are yours to own.

As the great philosopher Epictetus said, *"It's not what happens to you, but how you react to it that matters."* And Robert Anthony put it simply, *"When you blame others, you give up your power to change."* Taking responsibility is not about guilt or shame, it's about reclaiming your power. Research in psychology shows that people with a strong internal locus of control, those who believe they have control over their lives, experience less stress, higher well-being, and greater success. When you accept ownership, you activate your brain's prefrontal cortex, the area responsible for planning, decision-making, and emotional regulation. In other words, responsibility lights up your power centers. The moment you shift from blame to ownership, everything changes. You stop searching for heroes because you become your own. You stop being a victim and start being a victor. As Maya Angelou said, *"We may encounter many defeats but we must not be defeated."* You are the author of your story, the painter of your canvas, the captain of your ship.

So, own your choices. Heal on your terms. And remember, as Grandma always says, *"Honey, nobody can give you peace but you."*

It's okay to break.

It's okay to fall.

It's okay to lose direction.

It's even okay to be wrong.

What is *not* okay is to give someone else the steering wheel of your life.

This world is loud. Opinions are everywhere. Mistakes are inevitable. But your strength? It's in your ability to say: *"This is my life. I take responsibility. And I am committed to getting better, every single day."* So take responsibility, and take your power back.The life you're dreaming of? It begins with a choice.Your choice.

Daily Steps to Own Your Life and Heal

1. Start Your Day with a Moment of Truth

Before you rush into the world, take a quiet moment. Ask yourself, "What's mine to own today?" It might be a feeling, a reaction, or a choice you need to make. Writing it down helps, like leaving yourself a little love note to keep your heart honest.

2. Catch Your Blame-Thoughts and Gently Redirect Them

When you notice yourself thinking, "It's their fault," or "I can't because..." pause. Grandma says, "Sweetheart, blame is like a pair of old shoes comfortable but it won't take you far." Instead, ask, "What can I do differently?" Even small steps count.

3. Reflect Before Reacting

When emotions rise like a storm, don't sail straight into it. Take a deep breath (Grandma swears by three deep belly breaths), and ask, "Why am I feeling this way? What's underneath this?" This tiny pause is the doorway to choosing how to respond, instead of reacting on autopilot.

4. Say "No" Without Guilt

Setting boundaries is the ultimate act of self respect. Grandma says, "You can't pour from an empty cup." Practice saying no to things or people who drain you, even in small ways. Every "no" is a step toward your freedom.

5. Own Your Mistakes Like a Pro

Made a mistake? Good. That means you're trying. Instead of hiding or blaming, say quietly to yourself, "This one's on me, and I'm going to do better." Celebrate the courage to own it, that's real strength.

6. Feed Your Mind with Empowerment

Read, listen, or watch something that uplifts you daily. Quotes, books, podcasts, whatever fills your soul with reminders that you're capable, worthy, and in charge.

8. Remember, It's a Journey, Not a Sprint

Some days you'll slip, and that's okay. Grandma always says, "Even the tallest oak was once a little nut that held its ground." Be kind to yourself. Get up, dust off, and keep going.

IV
Shifting Your Mindset from 'Why' to 'What'

"You may not control all the events that happen to you, but you can decide not to be reduced by them."- Maya Angelou

Stop worrying, sugar. Ask better questions and you'll get better answers. Let's be honest: life doesn't always go the way we plan. Things fall apart, people disappoint us, and circumstances feel unfair. But here's what your grandma would gently remind you while pouring tea: sitting around asking "why" won't fix the situation or help you move forward. It's time to shift your focus from overthinking the problem to finding a way through it.

The Questions We Ask Shape the Life We Live

Questions are like steering wheels. Ask the wrong ones, and you'll crash into anxiety, guilt, or helplessness. Ask the right ones, and suddenly BOOM you're back in the driver's seat.

The Problem with "Why" Questions

Asking "Why did this happen to me?" or "Why can't I do better?" tends to drag you into emotional quicksand. These questions are backward-looking and self-critical. They can:

- Increase self-judgment and blame:
  "Why are you always late?" feels like a verbal slap, not a solution.
- Trigger guilt and rumination:
  "Why did I say that?" keeps you stuck in regret instead of growth.

- Dismiss others' emotions:
"Why can't you just move on?" sounds more like a demand than support.
- Ignite anxiety:
"Why can't I control this?" is often a cry from the heart but rarely a path forward.

As Viktor Frankl wrote in *Man's Search for Meaning*:
"When we are no longer able to change a situation, we are challenged to change ourselves."

Grandma's version?

"You can cry about the rain, or you can grab an umbrella and get to stepping."

Shifting to "What" Questions

"What" questions don't dwell, they *do*. They turn your brain toward *solutions*, not spirals. That's when the magic begins.

Instead of...

Ask...

"Why did this happen to me?"

"What can I do to move forward from this?"

"Why are they treating me like this?"

"What can I do to protect my peace?"

"Why do I always mess up?"

"What can I learn and do better next time?"

Ralph Waldo Emerson said: "What lies behind us and what lies before us are tiny matters compared to what lies within us."

And grandma? "What's done is done, sugar. Now go do something about it."

Overcoming the Illusion of Control

One major reason we spiral into "why" is because we want to control everything, people, plans, outcomes, even time. Newsflash: you can't even control how fast your rice cooks, much less people's behavior.

- People have free will. You can influence, but not force.
- Intent matters. Don't always assume malice where there's just misunderstanding.
- Life is unpredictable. Control what you can, and let go of what you can't.

Epictetus, the Stoic sage, said it best: "Make the best use of what is in your power, and take the rest as it happens."

The Psychology Behind This Shift

Cognitive Behavioral Therapy (CBT) teaches that *thoughts influence feelings, which influence behavior.* By switching from helpless "why"s to empowering "what"s, you activate your brain's problem solving mode and dial down emotional chaos.

- Mindfulness helps you observe thoughts without judgment, so you can pause and redirect them.
- Neuroplasticity shows that changing the questions you ask literally rewires your brain toward healthier thinking.
- Solution based strategies increase resilience and prevent mental paralysis.

Studies show people who break problems into small actions experience lower stress and greater confidence.

Neuroscience of Questions – Rewiring the Brain

Questions don't just reflect your mindset, they shape your brain. When you repeatedly ask negative "Why" questions, your brain strengthens neural pathways associated with stress, anxiety, and helplessness. But when you shift to "What can I do?", your brain activates the executive function regions responsible for planning and creative problem solving.

This shift creates dopaminergic responses, meaning your brain starts rewarding you with small doses of dopamine for progress, clarity, and hope. You literally feel better when you ask better questions.

"Your brain is a prediction machine. Give it better questions, and it will search for better futures." – Dr. Andrew Huberman

Existential Psychology – Responsibility Breeds Freedom

Existential psychologists like Rollo May and Irvin Yalom emphasize that asking "Why me?" often stems from a deeper fear of meaninglessness. In contrast, "What can I do?" places responsibility back in your hands and that's where freedom lives.

When you say "What now?" you're not just solving a problem; you're creating meaning from your suffering. And that makes you more alive, not less.

"He who has a why to live can bear almost any how." – Nietzsche

Metacognition – Becoming Aware of How You Think

Metacognition (thinking about your thinking) allows you to interrupt negative loops. When you feel stuck in "Why", practice a quick internal dialogue:

- "Is this question helpful?"
- "What emotion is it fueling?"
- "What question would serve me better?"

This is called a "cognitive reframe", a core skill in emotional intelligence and leadership development. It builds the muscle of mental flexibility, which is strongly linked to long term happiness and adaptability.

The Identity Shift – From Victim to Author

Asking "What can I do now?" is not just a question, it's a **statement of identity**. You're no longer just someone life happens to; you become someone who shapes life with intention.

This mindset is a cornerstone of narrative therapy, where people re-author their story by changing the language they use. You stop being the person who "got hurt" and become the one who "learned, adapted, and rose."

Spiritual Layer- Surrendering the Uncontrollable

We've touched on this already, but here's a deeper framing:
In many spiritual traditions (Christianity, Stoicism, Buddhism), the act of surrender isn't weakness, it's a conscious choice to trust in divine timing or higher intelligence.

Releasing the "Why" is a sacred act of faith. It's saying: *"Even if I don't understand it, I trust I'll grow through it."* That opens the heart, and invites peace.

The Transformation: From Stuck to Empowered

Changing "Why me?" to "What now?" flips the script. It's how you go from feeling stuck to becoming unstoppable.

Tony Robbins said: "The quality of your life is determined by the quality of the questions you ask."

Decluttering Your Thoughts

When you feel like your head is a tangled drawer of holiday lights, try this:

Step 1: Draw Two Columns

Column A: Things I Can Control
Column B: Things I Cannot Control
Write *everything* down. Be brutally honest.
Step 2: Let Go of Column B
Pray, meditate, take a walk, cry it out. Then breathe and release. Imagine grandma whispering,
Hand it to God, honey. He's got a bigger toolbox than you.
Step 3: Take Action on Column A

- Choose the *smallest possible action* you can take today.
- Build momentum, not pressure.
- Celebrate tiny wins like grandma celebrates a clean kitchen, loud and proud.

Reinhold Niebuhr's Serenity Prayer guides this mindset:
"God, grant me the serenity to accept the things I cannot change, courage to change the things I can, and wisdom to know the difference."

And remember, sugar, the quality of your questions depends on whether you're listening with your heart or just spinning in your head. So the next time life throws a curveball, and it will- pause. Take a breath. Don't get lost in the chaos. Instead, gently ask yourself:

"What can I do right now, with what I've got?" Because even if you can't rewrite the whole story, *you* can always turn the page. As William James states, the greatest discovery of my generation is that a human being can alter his life by altering his attitudes. While we can't always control life's winds, we can learn to sail with intention. And trust, your next chapter begins the moment you stop asking "why" and start choosing "what now. And if you ever forget, just imagine Sniffa grandma handing you a warm cup of chai, looking you in the eyes and saying, "You've got this, baby. Now turn the page."

"Life is 10% what happens to us and 90% how we react to it." – Charles R. Swindoll

Practical Steps to Shift Your Mindset and Take Control

1. Pause and Reflect:
   When faced with a challenge, take a deep breath. Instead of immediately asking "Why me?" pause and consciously choose to ask, "What can I do right now?"

2. Write it Down:
   Keep a journal or a notes app handy. Write down the situation and then list actionable steps you *can* take, no matter how small. This shifts your brain into problem solving mode.
3. Focus on What You Can Control:
   Divide your worries into two lists:

   - Things you can control
   - Things you cannot control
     Commit to letting go of the uncontrollable and focus your energy on what's within your power.

4. Set Small, Achievable Goals:
   Break your action steps into bite sized tasks. Even tiny progress matters and builds momentum toward bigger changes.
5. Practice Gratitude:
   Each day, write down three things you're grateful for. Gratitude helps reframe your mindset toward positivity and resilience.
6. Embrace a Growth Mindset:
   View setbacks as lessons, not failures. Ask, "What can this teach me?" and use the insight to grow stronger.
7. Repeat Affirmations:
   Remind yourself daily: "I have the power to choose my response." This reinforces your control over your attitude.

V

Cheat Your Mind And Set Yourself Free

"You become what you believe." – Oprah Winfrey

Baby, let me tell you something you might not hear from those fancy coaches or your social media scroll, sometimes, the best thing you can do for yourself is *lie*. That's right. Not to others, never to others, your word is sacred. But to your own stubborn, noisy little mind? Oh, you better lie your way to freedom if that's what it takes.

Because your mind? It's not as clever as it thinks it is. It don't care what's real. It cares what's repeated. You tell it you're worthless enough times, and it'll build a whole life around that lie. But you start feeding it a new story, "I'm healing," "I'm enough," "I'm coming back stronger" and suddenly, your life starts to turn. Like a sunflower toward the sun. This mind of yours is like an old record player. It'll play the same scratched-up song until you grab the needle and move it. And sometimes, baby, that means saying things you don't feel yet. You don't wait to feel confident before walking like a queen. You walk like a queen until your bones believe it. You don't wait for peace to feel still. You declare peace like you own it, even when the storm's at your front door.

Don't get me wrong, I ain't telling you to ignore your pain. Feel it. Cry it out. But don't you dare build a throne for it. Don't you dare make a God out of your grief. Feelings are messengers, not masters. Listen, then let them pass. You don't need to make a home in the heartbreak. I've watched too many good people waste their life talking about what they lost, what they hurt, what went wrong. That's planting weeds, honey. And then they wonder why their soul won't bloom. You want new results? You better plant new roots. And those roots,they start in the mind.

Let me tell you a little something I always told myself when I had nothin' but grit and a prayer: *"Say it until it feels like breathing."* That's not pretending. That's prophecy. That's declaring what's coming while your hands are still empty. Faith ain't about having. It's about *knowing*. And sometimes, it sounds like a lie to everyone else. Picture a prisoner. Four walls. Cold floor. Shame thick in his chest. The world already wrote him off. But what if he wakes up and whispers, "I still have breath. I still have a mind. I still got purpose." What if he picks up a pencil, a brush, a beat up Bible, and starts creating something beautiful? He just cheated his mind, darling. And in doing, he set his soul free.

You ever heard of Viktor Frankl? Survived the Holocaust. Saw hell firsthand. And still said, *"Everything can be taken from a man but one thing: the last of the human freedoms, to choose one's attitude."* Now *that* is the kind of man who knew how to cheat his mind and walk out free, even with chains on his feet.

Because here's the truth no one else will say to you with love and fire in the same breath: You're not stuck. You're just loyal to the wrong story. And it's time past time you write a new one.

So go on now. Lie to your mind if you have to. Call yourself whole even when you feel hollow. Walk like you're already free, even if the world still calls you broken. And if anyone asks, you tell them your grandma said: "Child, sometimes the only way out is to believe before you see."

Now lift your chin, and move like the future's already here.

The Coffee Trick and the Power of Belief

Let me tell you a little story, child.

Back in India, I used to drink tea and coffee like it was water,six, seven cups a night, sometimes even more. I'd sip on a strong cup after dinner and head straight to bed without a problem. I didn't toss, I didn't turn. I slept like a baby. Why? Because no one ever told me I shouldn't be able to sleep. I didn't believe caffeine kept you awake. And so... it didn't. Simple as that.

Then I moved to London. I started reading all those wellness blogs and seeing videos of fancy folks saying, "Don't drink coffee after 4 p.m., it'll wreck your sleep." Suddenly, I started believing it. And just like that, the same cup that once rocked me to sleep was now keeping me up, heart racing, eyes wide open at midnight.

Now, listen here, did the coffee change? No, ma'am. It was the same roasted beans, same cup, same warmth. *But the belief changed.* And once the belief changed, the body followed.

That's when I knew for certain: *your body listens to your mind, and your mind listens to your words.*
You say something long enough, truth or lie and your mind don't question it. It just follows orders.

So I thought, well, if my words can convince my body to stay awake, what else could they do?

I started saying something new: "I am beautiful." "I am young." "I glow from the inside out."

And let me tell you, no, my wrinkles didn't vanish overnight and my hair didn't suddenly curl like it used to in the '70s. But something far more powerful happened: *I started to feel beautiful.* I started walking with my shoulders a little higher, smiling without checking a mirror, looking people in the eye without wondering what they saw. And wouldn't you know it? The world started agreeing. Strangers complimented me. People said I had a glow about me. Not because my face changed, but because *my belief did.*

Sweetheart, let your Grandma remind you: *People will see you how you see yourself.* Walk like you're enough, and the world will echo it back. Walk like you're invisible, and they'll walk past you.

Because if a little coffee can obey your belief... imagine what the rest of your life could do.

Speak What Serves You
"As a man thinketh in his heart, so is he." – Proverbs 23:7
Now listen close, child. This one's important. You may not remember all the things I've told you over the years, but if you remember this, you'll save yourself decades of suffering:

Your thoughts are seeds. Your words are water. And your life, your joy, your pain, your peace that's the harvest. You keep telling yourself, "I'm unlucky. I'm tired. I'm broken. Nothing good ever happens to me," and guess what? Your mind, that loyal little servant of yours, will say, "Yes, ma'am!" and start planting weeds where flowers should be. And worse, it will start bending your world just to prove you right. Because your brain would rather be consistent than happy.

But here's the truth your Grandma learned the long, hard way: you can flip the script. You can speak life into the places where death tried to live. You can whisper strength into your bones even when they're shaking. You don't have to feel it to say it. And sometimes, most times you've got to say it before you feel it.

I've watched miracles grow from words. Real ones. I've seen tired, worn out women whisper to themselves, "I've still got something to give," and rise up to build businesses, raise families, heal bodies. I've seen men shattered by life say, "This pain is growing something strong in me," and go on to lead others through storms. Not because their pain disappeared, but because their perspective changed.

The Golden Rule: Feel, Then Flip

Now, don't you dare think I'm telling you to bottle up your feelings and smile through the storm like some porcelain doll. No, ma'am. You've got to feel it first. Sit with it. Cry if you must. Let your heart bleed honestly.

But don't you dare *marinate* in it. Pain is a place to *visit*, not to *build a home* in.

So here's what you do, baby. You feel... and then you flip.

Say it with me:

- "This feeling is valid, but it is not permanent."
- "This hurt is shaping something strong in me."
- "I choose to see this differently."

That's not pretending. That's *power*.

Even Seneca said, *"We suffer more in imagination than in reality."* And wasn't he right? Half the storms we drown in never even happen, they live only in our minds.

Reticular Activating System

Come closer, sweetheart, because this one's important, one of those things that can change your whole life if you really let it sink in.

Inside your brain, right near the stem where all the wires run like a big ol' switchboard, lives a little bundle of nerves called the **Reticular Activating System**, the RAS. Now don't let that name scare you off. Just think of it like a filter. A wise, quiet little doorman that decides what gets let into your conscious mind and what gets ignored. Because you, darling, are surrounded by **millions of bits of information** every second, sounds, sights, words, emotions, energies. And if your brain tried to focus on *all* of it, you'd short circuit in a second!

So the RAS does you a favor. It **filters reality based on what you believe, what you focus on, and what you say over and over.** That's right, baby, your brain is listening even when you think it's not. It's tuning itself based on your internal playlist. You tell it, "I'm unlovable," and it starts scanning the world to prove you right. It'll pick up the one person who ignored your message, the one day your outfit didn't hit right, the one time you fumbled your words. And then it'll whisper, "See? I told you."

But let me tell you a secret: you can flip the station. You start feeding your mind the words you wish were true like, "I am enough," or "I always find a way," or "The world is kind to me", and slowly, your RAS starts searching for *evidence* of that instead.

It's like tuning a radio, honey. Leave it on a static filled station and all you'll hear is noise. But twist that dial toward hope, and suddenly, sweet music starts playing where there was once only silence.

You want proof? Let me tell you about your Auntie Silkamma (we call her Siluku). She used to always say, "I'm terrible with money." And guess what? She was. Bills unpaid, pennies scattered. But when she started saying, "I'm learning how to manage money well,", just that small shift things began to turn. She started noticing free finance workshops. A neighbour offered her a budgeting book. She even found a forgotten savings account! Nothing magical, just her RAS showing her the doors that were always there but hidden behind the fog of her old belief.

Like **Wayne Dyer** used to say, "*When you change the way you look at things, the things you look at change.*" And like **Rumi** whispered centuries ago, "*What you seek is seeking you.*"

Your beliefs are like Google search terms for your life. You type in, "Why does no one love me?" and your brain will show you all the reasons. But if you search, "Why am I so deeply loved?", it'll dig up a whole new story. The facts of your life don't change. But the focus does.

So if you wouldn't plant it, don't say it.

Your mind is your garden, and RAS is your gardener. Give it weeds, it'll grow weeds. Feed it sunlight, and baby, you'll bloom. And when the doubt creeps in, because it will, just remind yourself:"*This is not truth, it's just habit. And habits can be changed.*"

Epigenetics: How Your Beliefs Speak to Your Body

"*Honey, your body listens when your soul speaks softly.*"

You see baby, for a long time folks thought our genes were like a fixed lottery ticket, whatever you got, that's what you're stuck with. But oh no, sweetheart, life's far more generous than that.

There's this field called **Epigenetics**, big word, I know but here's what it means in Grandma's kitchen talk: your thoughts, your feelings, the environment you live in, even the stories you tell yourself, can turn your genes on or off like little switches. It's like your mind holds the lamp, and your genes dance in its light or hide in its shadow.

When your thoughts are dark and heavy, worry, fear, anger they stir up stress inside your body. That stress isn't just in your head; it trickles down, bringing inflammation and illness along for the ride. It's like watering a garden with dirty water nothing good grows there.

But when you fill your heart with gentle, kind thoughts? When you tell yourself, "I am healing," or "I am strong," your body listens. It calms the storm. It starts repairing, renewing, and growing resilience you never knew you had.

Remember **Dr. Bruce Lipton**, a scientist who studied this? He said, *"Genes are not our destiny, but a blueprint that responds to the signals we send."* In other words, your beliefs are instructions to your body.

Let me tell you about Shakeela, my neighbour. She was always tired, stressed, and sickly. But when she started practicing calm breathing, saying kind words to herself each morning, and believing she could feel better, something shifted. Her energy returned, her doctor said her inflammation markers dropped, and she even started sleeping peacefully.

It's not magic, baby, it's biology dancing with belief. Treat yourself kindly, your cells are eavesdropping.

Grandma's Daily Magic: Simple Habits to Tell Your Body "You Got This"

1. Morning Mantra, Darling!
   Before you even open your eyes, whisper something good to yourself. Doesn't have to be fancy. Try, "Today is a blessed day," or "I will be around the kindest people ever." Your brain loves this little love note first thing.
2. Belly Breaths, Not Drama!
   When life feels like a soap opera, take a deep breath *all the way down to your belly.* Inhale slow, count to four, then breathe out. Repeat a few times and feel your body calm down. It's like a reset button!
3. Feed Your Soul (and Your Stomach)
   Eat something colourful, fresh, and real. Because your body is a temple, not a trash can! Plus, fresh food feeds those genes to be their best selves.
4. Smile, even if You're Alone!
   Smile in the mirror or to yourself like you just heard the best news ever.

Your brain can't tell the difference between a fake smile and a real one, and both send happy signals to your body. Trust me, it's cheaper than therapy !

5. Write Yourself a Love Letter

At night, jot down one thing you did well or one thing you love about yourself. Doesn't have to be Shakespeare "I didn't trust that guy today" counts! Your mind remembers what you praise, so heap on the kindness.

6. Move, Baby, Move!

Dance in your kitchen, stretch like a cat, or just wiggle your toes. Moving sends happy vibes to your cells and tells them you're alive and kicking. And don't worry if you look silly, Grandma's danced like a monkey and lived to tell the tale!

7. Turn Off the Drama News

Limit your daily dose of doom scrolling. Your mind is not a garbage dump. Protect your peace by choosing what you feed it.

VI

The Mind's Trick Mirror

Coping with Cognitive Distortions

Break the Mind's Illusions. Reclaim Your Power.

The Roots of Distortion

Oh, sweetheart, let me tell you, there's a full blown *telenovela* happening inside that pretty little head of yours, and honey, the villain isn't some mustache twirling stranger. Nope, it's your own dang voice, dressed up in a convincing disguise like it's auditioning for *Mission Impossible*.

Now, before you start thinking Grandma's gone off her rocker, let's talk facts. Back in the swinging '60s (when I was still turning heads, mind you), a brilliant man named **Dr. Aaron T. Beck**, aka the *Godfather of Good Thinking* pioneered the idea of **cognitive distortions**. That's just a fancy way of saying your brain sometimes lies to you like a politician during election season. His student, **Dr. David D. Burns**, took that ball and ran with it, writing *Feeling Good: The New Mood Therapy*, a book so powerful it could probably out-sell my famous rum cake (and that's something).

Here's the kicker, sugar:

"The way you think determines the way you feel." – **Dr. David D. Burns**

And his mentor, Dr. Beck, dropped this truth bomb:

"Change your thoughts, and you change your world."

Now, let's marinate on that like a good bourbon glaze. Your world doesn't crumble because life throws a tantrum, oh no, it crumbles because your brain starts narrating it like a bad horror movie. *"Oh no, I tripped in public, I'll never recover! Everyone's laughing at me!"* Pfft. Please. Half those people are too busy worrying about their own muffin tops to notice yours.

Here's a little historical fun fact to lighten the mood: Did you know that **Marcus Aurelius**, the OG Stoic philosopher (and let's be real, a total silver fox back in his day), said:

"You have power over your mind, not outside events. Realize this, and you will find strength."

Same wisdom, just wrapped in a toga instead of a lab coat.

So, darling, the next time your brain starts spinning drama like a daytime soap opera, remember you're the director of this show. And if this grandma can trade her knitting needles for a six-pack-armed boyfriend, you can sure as hell rewrite those mental scripts.

The Invisible Force Shaping Your Reality (And Grandma's No Nonsense Take on It)

Oh, sugar plum, let's have a real heart to heart about that three pound miracle between your ears, your mind. It's either your hype man, cheering you on like a drunk aunt at a wedding, or it's that backstabbing frenemy whispering doom like a bad weather report. And honey, it *believes* whatever you keep telling it.

Think about it how many times have you felt a tiny twinge in your knee and, after a quick Google dive, convinced yourself you've got some rare disease last seen in 18th-century sailors? *That*, my dear, is your brain playing telephone with reality. And just like that game, the message gets more ridiculous by the second.

Cognitive distortion is just a fancy term for your mind throwing a dramatic tantrum, like a toddler denied candy. It takes a papercut and turns it into an amputation. It hears silence and assumes betrayal. It's not *lying* to you it's just stuck in its own telenovela.

But here's the kicker, straight from Grandma's lips:

"What you're going through isn't always the problem. The story you're telling yourself about it is."

Boom. Let that sink in like a good moisturizer.

The ancient Stoics knew this, Epictetus said, *"Men are disturbed not by things, but by the views which they take of them."* And that man didn't even have WiFi to spiral with!

So next time your brain starts drafting its Oscar-worthy tragedy, pause. Ask yourself: *"Is this fact, or is this my fear doing stand-up comedy?"* Because, darling, you're not broken, you're just human. And humans? We've been catastrophizing since young.

Now, go pour yourself a drink (or a green juice), and rewrite that mental script. And remember if this grandma can laugh at her wrinkles while dating a man who still has his baby teeth, you can sure as hell laugh at your brain's melodrama.

Chin up, buttercup. Reality's what you make it.

Meet the Mind Traps: Major Cognitive Distortions (Grandma's Guide to Kicking Their Asses)

Listen up, buttercup, your brain's been playing dirty tricks on you, and it's time we called them out like bad behavior . These sneaky little saboteurs are the reason you stress eat when one thing goes wrong. Well, no more! Let's expose these mental gremlins one by one.

1. Filtering (The Drama Queen)

You could get ten "You're amazing!" texts and one "Meh," and guess which one you'll obsess over? Honey, that's like throwing away a diamond because it's not *flawless*. Even Michelangelo's David has a crooked pinky(google this its interesting), perfection is overrated.

Next time you fixate on the negative, imagine me smacking your wrist with a wooden spoon. Then, write down THREE good things that happened today. Yes, even "I didn't spill coffee on myself" counts.

2. Polarized Thinking (All-or-Nothing Nonsense)

Life isn't black and white, sweetheart, it's a messy, beautiful rainbow. Thinking in extremes (*"If I'm not perfect, I'm a failure!"*) is like saying my boyfriend is either Brad Pitt or a garbage fire. Reality check: He's somewhere in between, just like you.

Add "AND" to your vocabulary. *"I messed up AND I'm still learning."* See? Progress, not perfection.

3. Overgeneralization (The Doomsday Prophet)

One bad date and suddenly *"No one will ever love me!"* Puh-lease. By that logic, my first husband (may he rest in peace) would've meant all men snore like chainsaws. Spoiler: They don't.

Swap *"always"* and *"never"* for *"sometimes."* *"Sometimes things go wrong, and that's okay."*

4. Jumping to Conclusions (The Psychic Fraud)

"They didn't reply... they hate me!" Darling, unless you've got a crystal ball and a PhD in mind-reading, you're just guessing. And let me tell you, my bingo night predictions are more accurate.

Ask yourself, *"What's another possible explanation?"* Maybe they're busy. Or their phone died. Or they're just rude. Either way, it's not about you.

5. Catastrophizing (The End-of-the-World Committee)

A headache? Must be a brain tumor. A missed call? Clearly, someone's dead. Sweetie, your imagination should be writing horror novels, not ruining your day.

Play the *"So what?"* game. *"So what if it's true? What's the actual worst-case scenario?"* Usually, it's not that bad.

6. Personalization (The Martyr Complex)

"The party was boring? Must be my fault!" Honey, unless you personally unplugged the music and hid the alcohol, CHILL. The world doesn't revolve around you, and that's *freeing*.

Repeat after me: *"Not everything is about me."* Feels good, doesn't it?

7. Blaming (The Accountability Avoider)

"It's THEIR fault I'm unhappy!" Newsflash: You're handing them the keys to your happiness. Take 'em back.

Ask, *"What's MY part in this?"* Not to beat yourself up, just to reclaim your power.

8. "Should" Statements (The Guilt Trip)

"I should be further along by now." Says who? The ghost of expectations past? Life isn't a race, and if it were, you'd still be lapping everyone on the couch.

Replace *"should"* with *"could."* *"I COULD work on this... or I COULD take a nap."* Both are valid.

9. Emotional Reasoning (The Feeler-Not-Facter)

"I feel stupid, so I must be." Oh, honey, feelings are like my ex-husband's hairline, unreliable.

Separate facts from feelings. *"I FEEL embarrassed, but that doesn't mean I AM embarrassing."*

10. Global Labeling (The Harsh Judge)

"I failed, so I'm a failure." By that logic, I burned a dosa once, so I must be a terrible cook. (Spoiler: My dosa's are legendary.)

Add *"right now"* to the end. *"I failed... right now."* Temporary, not terminal.

11. Always Being Right (The Ego Trap)

"I can't be wrong, that would mean I'm worthless!" Sweetie, even Einstein admitted mistakes. And he had better hair than you.

Try saying, *"I might be wrong... and that's okay."* Feels scary, then freeing.

VII

Don't Die With Your Light Still In You

"Your calling is not just about you. It's about the lives connected to you through your obedience to it." -Priscilla Shirer

Let me ask you something, honey: what if the very thing the world has been waiting for, the light that could change everything, is locked deep inside your heart? Your voice, your story, your dreams, your very purpose all waiting quietly, ready to burst forth and heal not only you but others who desperately need what only you can give. You weren't made to live small or silent. No, you came into this world filled with brilliance and strength, wrapped in a light meant to guide, inspire, and lift others. Sometimes life tries to convince you to dim that light, to hide your fire so you don't make others uncomfortable. But I'm here to remind you, just like Grandma would, don't you dare make yourself smaller to fit into a world that wasn't built for your greatness.

As Dylan Thomas says, "Do not go gentle into that good night. Rage, rage against the dying of the light." Your light isn't some timid flicker; it's a blazing fire. And it's your sacred duty to keep it burning bright through every storm, every shadow, every lonely moment. Maya Angelou told us, "There is no greater agony than bearing an untold story inside you." What story are you holding back? What truth do you fear to share? Those unspoken words and hidden gifts, they're not just yours to keep. They're the keys to someone else's healing, the spark waiting to ignite courage and hope in a weary soul.

Remember what Grandma says, "If God put it in you, He means for it to be used. Don't waste what's been entrusted to you." Your gifts are seeds, baby, seeds meant to grow into mighty oaks that shelter and protect generations yet to come. Your light isn't decoration; it's divine purpose. It's a calling only you can answer. And Marianne Williamson's words ring true: "Our deepest fear is not that we are inadequate. Our deepest fear is that we are powerful beyond measure." You were created for power, for purpose, for greatness. So don't die with that power locked inside. Don't leave this world without unleashing your full light.

It's Not Just a Dream, It's a Calling

Now listen, sugar, finding your purpose ain't no Pinterest perfect moment where a golden light shines down and a choir sings "Hallelujah." No baby. It's more like wrestling with a stubborn mule in the middle of a thunderstorm, messy, loud, and downright exhausting. Most of the time, purpose doesn't tiptoe up to you wearing a fancy hat. Nope. It barges in like chaos wearing muddy boots, knocking over everything you thought you knew.

I didn't stumble onto my purpose all neat and tidy, wrapped up like some fancy gift with a bow. Lord no! I tripped over it, face-first, time and time again, through trials that felt like a soap opera, mistakes bigger than Grandma's boyfriends, failures that made me want to hide under the bed, and yes, a good few breakdowns that felt like my heart had been run over by a stubborn buffalo. But piece by piece, like Grandma patching up your favorite quilt, I found the thread that stitched it all together: helping people feel whole again, that is grandma's purpose.

I started working at 20, just a young girl with a shiny degree and a restless heart that wouldn't sit still. Now, at this age, well, let's just say my knees have a little more opinion on what I should be doing than I do! I've tried everything under the sun, language trainer, DJ spinning those old school tracks (don't ask me to twerk, honey, my back would file a complaint), professor, author, marketing admin you name it, I dabbled. From the stuffy world of corporate suits to the flashing lights of console decks. It looked like a mess to outsiders, like I was chasing butterflies in a tornado. But inside? Honey, it was a beautiful blueprint. Every time I helped someone feel seen, heard, or a little more healed, I felt like the best version of myself, like I'd just baked the perfect batch of cookies and they came out just right. So don't be afraid to mess up and change lanes a few times. Sometimes, the crooked roads lead to the sweetest destinations. And remember, your purpose? It ain't a straight line it's a wild dance, and you've got the rhythm inside you already.

From Pain to Power

Now listen here, sugar. I didn't become a teacher because I was some genius child prodigy, no, ma'am. I became a teacher because for a long time, I felt downright dumb. As a student, I wasn't the one throwing spitballs or causing a ruckus, I was invisible. Not the "cute troublemaker" kind of invisible, but the "nobody even sees me" kind. I wasn't a problem child, honey I was a child with problems.

Teachers didn't teach me, they branded me. Dumb. Not good enough. Worthless. I carried those ugly words like a worn out coat through many years, freezing in that cold shadow of self doubt. But then, just when I was about ready to give up, God sent me a teacher who changed everything. Now this man didn't just read the syllabus oh no, he read me. He taught me to believe in myself when no one else did. That right there? That was divine redirection, baby.

I realized if one teacher could save me from that dark place, then I wanted to be that light for someone else. When I finally stood at the front of the class, my mission was crystal clear: I wasn't just fixing grammar, I was fixing self-worth. Especially in a place like India, where your English can sometimes feel like a golden ticket or a rusty chain, I made sure every student knew this truth: Your worth is *never* measured by your accent or your vocabulary. Confidence isn't born in fancy words it's born in faith. I wanted every kid to walk out the door knowing, "I am enough. Exactly as I am."

Then, well, life got spicy. I fell in love with an extraordinary man a DJ. Now don't be fooled, I wasn't swept off my feet by his beats alone. No, no. What got me was his purpose. He told me once, "People carry heavy lives, but on the dance floor, they leave it all behind. A good DJ heals the room. The beat isn't just for the body it's for the soul."

Oh, honey, that got to me, in the best possible way. Watching him work was like seeing therapy disguised as music. Burdens lifted, spirits lifted, and me? Well, I wanted in. So I learned the craft, not to chase fame or flash, but to be part of that healing. To be someone's reason to smile, to dance, to breathe a little easier. That? That right there is purpose.

And then, there was the book. It wasn't a bestseller, and honestly, it wasn't supposed to be. It was raw. It was messy. It was brutal honesty on every page. I didn't write for applause, I wrote for the invisible ones. For those who never had the microphone, the spotlight, or even a moment to say, "Here I am." I poured my truth out, hoping someone, somewhere, would read it and feel just a little less alone. That? That is purpose.

And when the book's pages were drying, I started *Chai & Conversation*, a little online space where people could shed their fears, find their voice, and speak boldly. What started as a whisper grew into ripples some found courage, some clarity, some found their calling. And once again, honey, that's purpose.

All these pieces, the teacher, the DJ, the writer, the conversation starter came together in Lumina, my heart's revolution, *my light-breaking-through-the-darkness* project. A platform for women to break free from the mess, to rise wild, bold, and true. It took me ten years to get here, and let me tell you, I'd take every wrong turn and dead end all over again, because this ain't a job it's a divine assignment.

Now listen close to what Oprah says, because Grandma ain't lying: "When you step into your purpose, you don't just light up, you light up the world." And baby, I don't know about you, but I'm ready to set the whole world on fire.

If you're playing small, you're stealing from the world.

Baby, let me ask you something. What if you were meant to be a fashion designer, but fear stitched your confidence shut? That means some woman out there walks into the biggest day of her life feeling unsure because the dress only *you* could design never existed. What if you were born to be a lawyer, but self-doubt stopped you from even applying? Someone who deserved justice might never receive it, because you never showed up. What if you were destined to be a singer, but silence became your safety net? That means someone out there goes another day without the song that could've saved them.

Every calling is sacred. Every gift is divine. And every time you choose fear over faith, hesitation over action, you rob the world of something only you could give. Your purpose isn't just about you, it's about the lives connected to you, the people waiting on the other side of your courage. As Pastor Mike Todd once said, "Your purpose isn't about you. It's about the lives that need you."

Imagine if A.R. Rahman decided to play it safe. Imagine if Yuvan Shankar Raja let insecurity win. Imagine if Oprah never picked up the mic. Imagine if your favorite author never wrote a word. The world would be dimmer, less inspired, less healed, less whole. Now imagine you, your voice, your vision, your presence. What are you doing with it?

When you step into your purpose, you light a path for others to walk. You become proof that healing is possible, that dreams are real, that reinvention is not only allowed, it's necessary. You don't need to save the world. You just need to show up, fully and faithfully, in your corner of it. Because when you rise, others rise with you.

Don't die with your music still in you, as Wayne Dyer said. And don't die with your light still in you, as I'm saying to you right now. You were not created to blend in. You were born to set things in fire baby, hearts, ideas, legacies. You were chosen for something sacred. It's time to stop running from it and start running toward it. No more excuses. No more shrinking. No more silence. Someone, somewhere, is waiting for your courage to wake up their own. So go. Not when it's perfect. Not when you're ready. Go now.Because if not you, then who? If not now, then when? As Pablo Picasso said, "The meaning of life is to find your gift. The purpose of life is to give it away." So give it. Boldly. Bravely. Unapologetically. The world is waiting.

Self Determination Theory:

You see, darling, there's something deep inside all of us , something that wants to feel alive, useful, and loved. Two smart fellas, Edward Deci and Richard Ryan, looked into this and said there are three little things we all need to feel happy and whole.

First, we need *autonomy*. That's just a fancy word for feeling like we're in charge of our own lives, like we get to make our own choices and follow our own path. It's like when I let you choose your own clothes as a child even if your socks didn't match, you stood a little taller, didn't you? That's the power of autonomy.

Second, we need *competence*. Oh, my sweet one, that means feeling like you're good at something that you're capable and strong. You know that warm glow you get when you do something well, even a small thing? That's your spirit saying, "Look at me, I can do this."

And finally, we need *relatedness*. That's just our human need to feel close to others, to love and be loved, to feel like we're part of something bigger than ourselves. It's like when the whole family sits around the table, and we laugh, share stories, and pass the food around, it fills more than just our bellies, doesn't it?

Now when you live with purpose, when you wake up each morning with meaning in your heart, you naturally feed all three of those needs. You make your own choices (autonomy), you use your God-given gifts (competence), and you help or connect with others (relatedness). And just like that, you don't just exist, you *inspire*.

That, my dear, is the beautiful science behind a purposeful life. Grandma may not have had the fancy words, but she always knew, when you live from your heart, everything else falls into place.

Neuroscience

You know, sweetheart, our brains are just like little gardens, whatever we plant and water, that's what grows. And science now shows something truly beautiful: when you live with purpose, real, deep-down meaning in your life your brain lights up in the happiest ways.

There's a special part of your brain called the *ventromedial prefrontal cortex*, oh, don't mind the big name, sugar. Just think of it as the part that helps you feel meaning, joy, and worth. When you do something that matters to you maybe helping someone, creating something, or following a dream that part of your brain says, "Oh yes, this is good." It's like a warm light flicking on inside your head.

And then there's something called *dopamine*. That's your brain's little happy dance chemical. It keeps you moving forward, especially when life gets tough. When you have purpose, your brain sends out more of this lovely stuff it's like giving you a gentle push from behind, whispering, "Keep going, darling. You're doing something important."

So even when the world feels heavy, or when things don't go your way, a sense of purpose helps you stand tall. It keeps you motivated and strong, not just in your heart, but right there in your brain, too.

Logotherapy

Now listen closely, sweetheart, because this is something every soul needs to hear. Life, as beautiful as it is, can sometimes feel like a storm, with winds that shake you and nights that seem too long. But do you know what gets you through those times? A sense of *meaning*. A reason. A "why" that burns like a little candle, even in the darkest room. There was a wise man named Viktor Frankl, a doctor, a thinker, and a survivor of the holocaust so cruel it broke many spirits. But not his. He lost everything, yet he held onto something no one could take from him: his purpose. He called it *Logotherapy*, and it means that if you have a reason to keep going, something you live for you can endure even the heaviest of burdens.

He said, "Those who have a *why* to live can bear almost any *how*." Isn't that something? It means your heart, your dreams, your love they all give your struggles meaning. Your pain isn't wasted, darling. It becomes part of your strength, part of your story. You learn to carry it with grace, like a warrior wrapped in gentleness.

Ah, come here, sugar, and let me share a little heart-to-heart with you, the kind that comes with years of watching life unfold. You see, from the very beginning of time, we humans weren't just made to eat, sleep, and get by. No, no, deep inside each of us is a beautiful, natural longing to *give something back*, to make a little ripple in the world before we go. That's not just poetic, it's in our biology. It's how we're *wired*. Just like how birds build nests and bees make honey, we're made to *contribute*, to love, to build, and to pass something meaningful on.

Some folks do it by raising kind-hearted children. Others leave behind stories, songs, ideas, or acts of kindness that ripple through generations. Whether it's through family, work, or simply a helping hand, that urge to leave the world just a little better than we found it? That's purpose, my darling.

Daily Practical steps:

1. Morning "Mission Whisper"

Before you roll out of bed, whisper to yourself:

"What's one lovely thing I can do today?"

Even if it's watering a plant or texting "I love you" that's purpose, baby.

2. Make someone smile

Purpose doesn't need a grand stage. Compliment someone's earrings. Leave a compliment or kind note in a strangers stuff. Tell your barista their smile is contagious.

3. Learn one tiny thing

Read a quote. Listen to a 2-minute podcast. Flip through a random page in a book. Feeding your brain = feeding your sense of purpose.

4. Tend to something living

Water your plant. Pet your dog. Smile at the tree outside your window.

Nurturing anything, even a cactus, reminds you: *you matter to something.*

5. "Tiny Wins" Journal

At night, jot down 1 thing that felt meaningful.

Example: *"Helped granny carry groceries."*

Your heart will remember: *"I did good today."*

6. Cook or prepare with love

Make your tea extra cozy. Plate your snack like it's a mini art show.

Why? Because when you treat small things like they matter, they start to feel like they do.

7. Hug with full presence

When you hug someone, hold them like you *mean it*. Feel your warmth transfer.

That's purpose in action: *"I'm here, and I care."*

8. Be a little light

Smile at the mailman. Wave at a baby. Say thank you with your eyes.

You never know whose cloudy day you just brightened.

9. Speak sweetly to yourself

Catch a mean thought? Gently say, *"Nope, we don't do that here. I'm doing my best."*

Self kindness is sacred. So is your voice.

When you live with that sense, that what you do *matters* it lights a fire in your belly and puts strength in your step. It's not about being famous or grand. Sometimes, just loving well and living kindly is the legacy. That's your soul saying, "I was here. I gave. I mattered."

So don't think your dreams or your heart's whisperings are silly. They're part of that ancient rhythm inside you that old, wise instinct to *make a difference*. And believe me, sweetheart, the world needs what only *you* can give.

The Inner Work – Healing and Rebuilding This section focuses on cultivating inner peace, emotional strength, and personal authenticity.

VIII

The Strength in Stillness- Choosing Response Over Reaction

"Between stimulus and response, there is a space. In that space is our power to choose our response. In our response lies our growth and our freedom." -Viktor E. Frankl

Let's get this straight: God made oceans wide and deep, not so we could cry ourselves into saltwater puddles every time someone misunderstood us. And yet, here I am, a strong, self-aware woman, with tear ducts that seem to throw a full-blown symphony the moment I try to explain myself. Not because I'm weak. Not because I'm fragile. But because somewhere along the way, being understood became survival. I cry. Often. Not out of pity or drama, but because when I speak from my heart, I feel from it too. One word, one misjudgment, one sharp tone from someone I love, and suddenly I'm no longer explaining, I'm unraveling. It's like standing in a courtroom without armor, hoping the world understands your truth before your voice cracks.But here's what I've learned: Tears do not disqualify strength. Sensitivity is not shameful. And being emotional doesn't mean you're broken, it means you're beautifully alive.

This chapter isn't about crying, it's about reclaiming what it means to feel deeply without apologizing for it. It's about the wisdom in pausing before explaining, and the power of not needing to prove yourself to those who love you. Because the real work, the hard and holy work, isn't just learning how to be strong. It's learning how to be soft without falling apart.

And from this space this stillness in the storm came brutal but beautiful truths from my boyfriend that changed how I see myself.

This is not a habit, it's a wound.

This isn't just a habit, baby, it's a wound. I told him I hated how I cried when I tried to speak my truth. And he didn't try to fix it with some Instagram quote wisdom or tell me to "just breathe." No. He looked me straight in the eye, and asked me a question that didn't just sting, it peeled the bandaid off something I didn't even know was still bleeding: "Were you always appreciated for who you were? Or only when you performed well?" Now listen. I've been through a lot, but that question? That one knocked the wind out of me. Because the answer came without thinking. Like it had been waiting in the hallway all this time, tapping its foot.

I've always worked harder than everyone around me. Not just for praise. Not just to get ahead. But to be seen. To be enough. Somewhere along the way, I learned that simply being good wasn't good enough. I had to be better. I had to earn love. And let's be honest, love given conditionally doesn't feel like love. It feels like a job interview you keep showing up for, hoping this time you'll finally be hired full-time.

That's why when someone dislikes me even a little it doesn't just brush past me. It burrows. I don't just hear "I disagree" I hear "You are not enough." I don't just feel misunderstood, I feel unworthy. And darling, that right there? That's not over-sensitivity. That's the echo of a little girl inside me still trying to be picked for the team.

You weren't born crying for attention. You were born crying to be held. Don't confuse the two. And Lord knows, I did. I thought if I worked hard enough, impressed them enough, stayed quiet enough, they'd see me and clap. But I didn't want applause, I wanted affection. I wanted to be held, not handled. So now, as a grown woman with bills, boundaries, and better eyeliner, I'm learning this: Love isn't earned like a paycheck. It's received like a gift. And if someone makes you work for it like a full-time job with no benefits, that's not love, that's emotional labor.

It's no wonder rejection cuts so deep, it's not just about now. It reopens that same old wound:

"Maybe if I was better, they'd love me." But no, baby. Not anymore. Because Grandma would look you in the eye and say: The people who matter will love you for showing up, not for showing off. So stop auditioning for roles in people's lives who haven't even earned front-row seats in yours.

It's Not Always About You, Sugarplum.

Now this one stung. The kind of sting that makes you blink slow, like someone just smacked you with a velvet slipper soft, but still hits like truth. We were talking about my reactions, and I was deep in my usual loop, overthinking, overanalysing, over-everything. And then he hit me with the grown up version of a bucket of cold water:

"How much do you think people actually think about you?" Oof. That one hit right between the ego and the insecurity. "You take people too personally," he said. "Sometimes people's actions have nothing to do with you. Their reactions reflect their mood, their wounds, their day, their values. Not yours." Now listen, I was about to be defensive, until I realized he wasn't attacking me. He was freeing me. Because the truth is, I'd been walking around like the emotional sun of the universe, thinking everything revolved around my feelings. Someone didn't text back? Must be mad at me. Someone snapped? I must've upset them. Someone's tone was off? What did I do wrong?

But the reality? People are living in their own messy, beautiful, complicated stories. Sometimes they're moody because their mom yelled at them, or they skipped breakfast, or Mercury's in retrograde and their phone died. It's not always about me. That was humbling. Because when you're an empath, or someone who's deeply self-aware, you start to believe that your ability to feel deeply makes you responsible for everything around you. But Grandma would look into your eye and say: Baby, you're not the main character in everyone else's soap opera. Sometimes you're just the lady throwing garbage in the background.

And you know what? That's actually liberating. Realizing the world doesn't revolve around my every reaction, every mood, every tender nerve, that's not rejection. That's relief.It means I can stop monitoring every glance, every pause, every shift in tone like a security guard watching 10 screens at once. It means I can finally breathe.It means I can start responding to life with curiosity instead of guilt.

So now, when something feels off, instead of panicking

I pause.

I sip my tea.

I ask myself, "Could this possibly have nothing to do with me?"

And 9 times out of 10, the answer is a big ol' YES. So Sweetheart, not everything's a personal attack. Sometimes people are just hangry. Let it go, bless their heart, and go drink your own damn tea."

Defense is a card you should use only 2% of the time.

Let's get one thing straight: you do not owe anyone an explanation for simply being you. Not for your choices. Not for your boundaries. Not even for your silence.

That constant itch to explain yourself? That's not clarity, it's a craving to be understood. But here's the kicker: the more you try to explain, the less seriously people tend to take you. It's like trying to convince someone the sky is blue while they've got their eyes closed. Exhausting, and pointless. And Grandma would tell you with one raised brow :

"If you gotta explain yourself every time you breathe, baby, you're talking to the wrong people."

You think you're helping them understand, but you're often just draining your spirit dry. Why? Because the more you defend, the more you doubt yourself. And people can smell that uncertainty. They don't hear your heart, they see the tears, the stumble, the emotional unravelling, and boom, they miss the message entirely.

As brutal as it sounds, many folks don't have the emotional capacity to see past your emotion. Let's be real: if you cry while trying to express your truth most will not lean in to understand. They'll lean away, uncomfortable, misjudging your softness as weakness. And that's a hard pill to swallow when you just wanted to be heard.

Benjamin Disraeli wasn't playing when he said: "Never complain. Never explain. "Sometimes, the most powerful, most graceful, most gangster move you can make is to say less. Let them think what they want. Let them misquote you, misjudge you, twist your silence into something scandalous. Let them make a soup out of scraps of your story. Because here's the truth bomb: You are not here to make everyone comfortable with who you are.

You know who you are. You know what you stand for. And you don't need to turn your truth into a TED Talk every time someone raises an eyebrow. Sugar, defence is a seasoning, not a main course. Sprinkle it when it's life or death. Otherwise, keep your peace and your pretty mouth shut." You do not owe anyone an explanation of who you are, or why you did what you did. The need to over-explain is often a desire to be understood, but ironically, it makes people take you less seriously. How you communicate matters more than what you say. People will remember how you made them feel. If you cry while explaining your truth, many will miss the point entirely. That's harsh. But real.

"Never complain, never explain."- Benjamin Disraeli

Sometimes, the most powerful thing you can do is say less.Let people misunderstand you. Let them judge. Let them form opinions based on fragments of your truth. You know who you are. You know what you stand for.

A Real Life Shift

There was this one day, Lord have mercy! I was boiling. Not the cute "simmering on the stove" kind of boiling, no. I was full-on pressure cooker, one whistle away from emotional explosion. Some man had scammed me. Lied and danced away with my deposit like it was Monopoly money. I was ready to set the world on fire, starting with his inbox. I typed a message so fierce it could've peeled paint off the wall: "You dishonest, value-lacking, two bit excuse for a human being may your Wi-Fi be slow for eternity." I was locked, loaded, and my thumb was hovering over send like a trigger.

But then... my boyfriends voice showed up in my head, uninvited as usual: "You wanna fight dirty with a pig, sweetheart? Guess what you both end up muddy, but the pig enjoys it."So instead of hitting send, I threw the phone on the bed, walked into the kitchen, and started cooking like I was trying to win Cook with Comali out of spite.

Fifteen minutes into stirring curry something started to shift. The fire was still there, but it had mellowed. I started thinking, "What if he didn't scam me out of cruelty, but out of desperation?" What if lying is just how he's survived his whole life? What if this actually had nothing to do with me?

I had two options:

-React from pain, and become just like him.

-Respond from strength, and become someone my boyfriend would brag about to my Mother in Law who is almost the same age as me (don't judge grandma now !).

So I deleted the rage text (with a dramatic sigh), and typed this instead: "You know the truth. Live with it. God bless you." It wasn't about letting him win. Please. My boyfriend didn't raise a doormat. It was about me not losing myself over someone who clearly already had. And honestly, it wasn't even that much money. It was the principle that had my blood pressure doing backflips. But giving away my peace over some man with the ethics of a soggy biscuit? Not worth it.

Like Elizabeth Kenny said:"He who angers you, conquers you."And Grandma would add: "...and baby, we don't hand out crowns to clowns."

The Power of the Pause

Here's the sacred truth:

Not everything needs a reaction. Not every fool deserves an audience. And not every hurt needs a press release. Sometimes, silence is not avoidance, it's strategy. Sometimes, stepping back isn't weakness, it's wisdom.

When we pause, when we breathe, and simply wait, we give ourselves the gift of coming home. Back to our calm. Back to our clarity. Back to the version of ourselves that isn't hijacked by hurt or ego. We stop reacting out of instinct, and start responding from intention. That's where our power lives. Crying isn't weakness. Feeling isn't failure. It's human. But wisdom is knowing when to cry, how to express, and if it even needs to be said out loud. Some things deserve tears, yes. But not all emotions need the center stage. You get to choose when and where you bleed. That choice, that pause is your strength.

As Viktor Frankl once said, "Between stimulus and response, there is a space. In that space is our power to choose our response. In our response lies our growth and our freedom."

Some of the strongest people I've ever met are the quietest in the storm. They don't throw words like weapons. They hold their peace like royalty. They don't explain themselves to people committed to misunderstanding them. They walk away with their head held high, heart unshaken, and soul intact. That's not indifference, that's power.

Sometimes the best clapback is no clap at all. Let God, karma, and their own guilt handle the rest. Now go stir that pot and save your voice for someone who deserves it. Growth is learning that silence can be louder than shouting.That walking away can be braver than confrontation. That stillness is not passivity, it's a superpower.

Maya Angelou said it best:

"You may not control all the events that happen to you, but you can decide not to be reduced by them."

Let them misjudge you. Let them form their opinions. Let them whisper, assume, question. That's not your weight to carry. You don't owe them clarity. You owe yourself peace. And peace is never found in the heat of reaction. It lives quietly in the stillness of thoughtful response. So the next time the fire rises in your chest and your fingers itch to react, pause. Choose power. Choose grace. Choose you.

Science and Psychology Behind Feeling this way:
Emotional Reactivity vs. Emotional Regulation

Alright, darlin', here's the deal in good old Grandma talk:

You know how sometimes when you get all riled up, like when someone says something that just pokes your heart the wrong way, your brain feels like a wild horse runnin' off without a rider? That's your amygdala the tiny but mighty alarm bell inside your brain's emotional clubhouse. It's the one that shouts, "Danger! Danger!" and makes you want to either fight, run, or well... sometimes just burst into tears like a leaky faucet.

Now, the prefrontal cortex, that's the sensible, calm grandparent of your brain. It's the one who says, "Hold on, child, let's think this through before we throw the whole tea pot out the window." But here's the tricky part: that grandparent takes a bit longer to get involved because it's busy making sure things are done right, like knitting a sweater or balancing the checkbook.

So, when you feel hurt or misunderstood, that little alarm bell (the amygdala) jumps in first, waving its arms and setting off fireworks. It makes your emotions flood out like a busted dam, crying, feeling shaky, or wanting to shout. And by the time the wise grandparent in your brain gets around to calming things down, you're already knee deep in the storm.

Daniel Goleman, who knows a thing or two about brains, calls this "amygdala hijack." It's like your emotions have stolen the steering wheel and are driving you wild. The good news? It usually takes about 20 minutes (or a cup of strong tea) for that calm grandparent to step in, take the reins, and help you respond with a little more grace and less waterworks.

So, the next time you feel that flood coming on, just remember: it's okay to let the amygdala shout for a bit, but be patient and let the wise prefrontal cortex take over before you send that text or start that explanation. I would say: Don't throw your hat in the fire when it's just a little smoke.

Attachment Theory:

Alright, sugar, you know how sometimes when you try to explain yourself, the tears just start sneaking out like little troublemakers? Well, that ain't no sign of weakness, it's your body's way of letting out all that built up stress and worry.

Now, here's a little wisdom from some fancy folks named John Bowlby and Mary Ainsworth. They came up with something called Attachment Theory, which is just a big way of saying: if as a kid you felt like you had to jump through hoops, like doing somersaults or perfect chores to be loved or accepted, then your grown up brain still remembers that. So when someone looks at you sideways or misunderstands you, your nervous system goes, "Oh no! This means I'm not loved anymore!" And your whole body hits the panic button.

So when you're explaining yourself, you're not just telling a story you're hoping, praying even, that the person hears your heart and still loves you. That's a lot to carry.

And here's the silver lining: crying is actually your body's built-in medicine cabinet. When tears flow, your body releases little helpers called oxytocin and endorphins, think of them as your own homemade chill pills. They calm you down, soothe your nerves, and help you feel better. For folks who are extra sensitive or empathetic, crying is just a natural way to show you're real, honest, and maybe just a little overwhelmed not that you're broken or weak.

So next time the tears come, just remember, honey: it's your body's way of saying, "I'm working through this." And that's a whole lot stronger than it looks.

The Urge to Defend:

Baby, you know how sometimes when you get all flustered, you start talking way more than you need to? Like you're trying to prove you're not the bad guy, explaining every little thing, hoping to make everyone happy? Well, that's called the Fawn Response, and it's one of those sneaky ways our brain learned to keep us safe when things were tough as kids.

See, when trouble showed up, some folks don't fight, don't run, and don't freeze up. Instead, they try to please everyone by being extra nice, over explaining, and bending over backwards. It's like saying, "Look at me, I'm good! Don't be mad!" all the time.

Why? Because maybe, just maybe, love back then felt like a game of "do this right, get love." It wasn't just "I love you no matter what." So, this habit of over-explaining is really your inner child's way of saying, "I'm scared if I don't say enough, or say it right, I won't be loved." Now, grown up you knows better. You don't owe anyone endless explanations just to keep peace. But that old habit? It's sticky like grandma's honey cake it takes time to peel away. And that's okay. Recognizing it is the first step to learning how to protect your heart without wearing yourself out with words.

How to Stop Over-Explaining and Protect Your Peace

1.Pause Before You Speak

When you feel the urge to explain everything, take a deep breath. Count to three like you're waiting for the kettle to boil. Give yourself a second to decide if you really need to say all that or if silence might be your best friend for now.

2.Keep It Simple, Sugar

Practice saying your truth in just a few clear words. None of that "I did this because…" or "But actually, what I meant was…" Keep it short, sweet, and to the point.

3.Write It Out, Then Let It Go

If your heart's all tangled up, write down what you want to say. Get it all out on paper or your phone. Then read it, but don't feel like you have to share the whole letter every time. Sometimes just getting it out helps the panic ease up.

4.Remember: You Don't Owe an Explanation

Practice saying, "I don't have to explain myself" out loud. Feel that in your bones. It's okay to protect your peace and keep some things for your own ears only.

5.Set a "Talking Limit"

Give yourself a friendly timer, like, "I'm only going to say three sentences about this." When you hit that limit, you pause and listen or walk away. It's like portion control, but for your words.

6.Ground Yourself in the Moment

When you feel those old worries creeping up, plant your feet on the floor and wiggle your toes. Say, "I'm safe right now." Sometimes your body needs to hear that just as much as your heart does.

7. Practice Saying "No" to Over Explaining

Next time you catch yourself trying to explain too much, smile and say, "I think that's enough for now." You're training your brain to chill out and trust that your simple words are enough.

8. Ask Yourself: "Is This My Battle?"

Before you launch into explanations, ask, "Do I really need to defend this? Or can I just let it be?" Most times, honey, the answer is to let it be.

9. Celebrate Your Wins

Every time you hold back the flood of words and keep your cool, give yourself a little nod or a "Well done, me!" Even Grandma would clap for that.

IX

Stress: Grandma's Wisdom on Turning Pressure into Power

"Stress is not what happens to us. It's our response to what happens. And response is something we can choose."-Maureen Killoran

Now listen here, sugar. Stress is like mirch masala in your curry. Just the right amount? It'll light up your senses, bring you alive, make the whole dish sing. But too much? Ayy haye! Your tongue's on fire, your eyes are watering, and you're questioning all your life choices. But don't go blaming the curry, honey. You're the one holding the spoon. Life doesn't always choose the spice level, you do. And how you stir that pot? That's where the real magic lies.

Stress, bless its heart, ain't the villain we make it out to be. It's a loud messenger in a sparkly outfit waving its arms and shouting, *"Darlin', something needs your attention!"* You see, it tends to show up when you're doing too much, too fast, or trying to carry what was never meant to be yours in the first place. And sometimes? It's there because life sees more in you than you're letting on. Back in my day, we didn't have fancy apps or breathing techniques in cute fonts. We had rocking chairs, long walks after supper, prayers whispered on the porch, and folks who listened without checking their watches. And you know what? That helped more than all the apps combined.

Stress isn't always bad. Sometimes it's what the smart folks call *eustress*, the good kind. It's that little flame under your behind that gets you moving before a deadline, the butterflies before a big speech, the stretch before a breakthrough. It's like kneading dough, you gotta press and fold and work it for the chappati to rise. No pressure, no rise. But don't get it twisted, ignore that stress too long, and it turns from helper to hindrance. That's when it becomes *distress*, and baby, that's when Grandma comes in with her no-nonsense spoon and reminds you to sit yourself down.

"The greatest weapon against stress is our ability to choose one thought over another."
-William James

Now hush for a moment and lean in close. Stress ain't the big bad wolf come to blow your house down. Sometimes, it's a whisper from your own spirit saying, *"Baby, you've got more inside you. More strength. More clarity. More potential."*

See, stress rarely knocks when you're coasting. It shows up when you're growing when you're stretching toward something better, deeper, higher. That's when it taps you on the shoulder like a no-nonsense coach saying, *"You in or you out?"*

And that's your cue, not to panic, but to pause. To sit with yourself and ask the kind of questions that sting just a bit but open the door to healing:

- Did I show up prepared or just wing it?
- Is this stress coming from the situation, or from how I'm reacting?
- Did I let someone who doesn't pay rent in my heart steal my peace?
- Am I choosing my actions, or just reacting like a pinball in a machine?

That, sweetheart, is where your power lives in that quiet little space between what happens and how you respond. Viktor Frankl called it "freedom." Grandma just calls it *wisdom*.

And let me be honest with you, most of the time, stress isn't about the world being unfair, it's about not having a plan. It's about staying up too late, waking up too tired, saying yes to everything, and trying to please folks who wouldn't notice if you disappeared for a week. Then your phone's buzzing, your to-do list is growing like weeds, and before noon you're already out of breath. That ain't life, baby that's you handing over the reins.

But you can take 'em back.

Start with this: make yourself a plan. Nothing too fancy. Just three clear goals for the day. Drink your water. Take a breath before you answer that message. Get up and stretch. Rest when your body whispers instead of waiting until it screams.

Remember:

- You are not your stress. It's a signal, not your identity.
- Control what you can, and hand the rest over to God.
- Rest is a requirement, not a luxury. You can't pour from an empty kettle.
- Boundaries protect your peace. Saying no doesn't make you mean, it makes you wise.

And baby, don't go expecting overnight miracles. You don't dig up a seed every morning to see if it's grown. You water it. You wait. You trust. Same goes for your goals and dreams. That business you're building? That degree? That healing you're chasing? It's working, even when you can't see it yet. Be patient. Keep going. Keep believing.

And here's Grandma's golden trick: when stress comes knocking, pause. Breathe. Ask yourself, *"What is this really about?"* Sometimes it's fear, sometimes it's fatigue, sometimes you just need a snack and a nap. Don't believe every thought that pops into your head. Some are just noise. Smile politely, say *"Not today,"* and sweep them right out like dust on the porch.

Psychological Theories of Stress

Baby, you think stress is only about what's happening around you? No, no, real stress begins in how you see what's happening. Just like how some people see rain and feel peace, and others see it and worry about muddy shoes, it's all in the mind's eye.

Let me tell you about a famous pair, **Lazarus and Folkman**, like two wise old village elders who understood the human heart. They said: it's not the big lion outside the hut that causes stress, it's whether you think that lion can reach you or not. First comes **Primary Appraisal** your brain asks, "Is this going to harm me? Is this trouble?" Then comes **Secondary Appraisal**, like your inner voice asking, "Can I handle this? Do I have the tools, the strength, the people?"

If your heart answers, "Yes, I can deal with it," then stress is like a mosquito, annoying, but not dangerous. But if you think, "Oh no, this is too much, I can't cope," then even a small issue feels like a mountain, and that's when stress grows heavy, like a sack of wet rice on your back.

Now let's talk about another wise man **Hans Selye**, who gave us the **General Adaptation Syndrome**. He said our body reacts to stress in three stages.

1. **Alarm Stage**: That's the moment your body hears trouble, your heart races, your muscles tense, like a cat that's just spotted a dog.
2. **Resistance Stage**: You hold your ground, keep doing your chores, your studies, your duties, even if you're tired. You're trying to push through.
3. **Exhaustion Stage**: But baby, no one can keep carrying a heavy pot forever. Eventually, you get worn out. Your body says, "I can't anymore," and that's when illness, sadness, and burnout start creeping in.

So remember, stress isn't always about the storm outside, it's about the strength of your inner shelter. And that shelter? It's made of understanding, faith, support, and the belief that you can handle life, one day at a time.

Neurochemistry of Stress

Honey, stress isn't just about your heart racing or your shoulders aching , no no, it messes with your brain's inner kitchen too! You know how when the kitchen has too much fire, everything starts to taste off? That's exactly what happens inside your brain when stress takes over.

Now, the head chef in this situation is cortisol, a stress hormone. In small doses, cortisol is helpful, like a strong chai in the morning. It wakes you up, helps you focus, and gives your brain some extra power to deal with the day. But if you keep drinking that chai all day, every day? Eventually, your nerves get jittery, your sleep goes for a toss, and your poor body feels worn out. Same with cortisol, too much of it over time can shrink your hippocampus (that's the little library in your brain that stores memories and helps you learn new things). So, if you're wondering why you keep forgetting your phone or can't study properly when you're stressed , now you know why!

Then there's serotonin and dopamine, the two sweet shopkeepers in your brain who keep you happy and motivated. When stress kicks in, these two close their shops, and boom, you start feeling low, irritable, even hopeless. That's why stress can lead to sadness or full-blown depression and anxiety.

And don't forget norepinephrine, it's like a night watchman who keeps you alert. But if he's on duty *all the time*, he becomes too loud, too jumpy you start feeling anxious, panicky, can't sleep properly, and always feel like something's about to go wrong.

So, my dear, your brain is like a delicate recipe. A bit of stress adds flavor, keeps you sharp. But if these brain chemicals go out of balance, it's like too much salt in kheer, spoils everything. That's why rest, prayer, peace, and good company are just as important as hard work.

The Role of Perception in Stress

Let me tell you something important .

Imagine a young girl about to speak in front of a crowd. One child might think, *"What if I forget my words? What if they laugh at me?"* and her stomach tightens, her hands tremble. But another child steps up with a sparkle in her eye and thinks, *"Finally! They'll hear what I have to say!"* Same stage, same audience, different story inside the heart.

This difference is shaped by many things, your past experiences (did someone once mock you or cheer for you?), your upbringing (were you taught to take risks or play it safe?), and your culture (were you told to speak up or stay quiet?). All these are like spices in your thinking, they flavor how you taste stress.

Now, wise people those psychologists in big glasses use what's called Cognitive-Behavioral Therapy (CBT). It's like giving your inner voice a new lens to see through. They don't try to remove the stressor, no no, they help you *change your story about it.* Instead of saying *"I can't handle this,"* you learn to say *"This is hard, but I've handled hard before."* That's called reframing, and it's as powerful as turning sour lemons into sweet pickle.

So remember this baby, stress isn't always about what happens to you, it's about the meaning you give to it. When you change the way you look at things, the things you look at begin to change. That's not just psychology that's wisdom passed from grandmother to grandchild for generations.

Stress and the Mind-Body Connection

Now listen sweetpie, your mind and your body? They don't live in separate houses. No, no. They're neighbors who share a wall what one feels, the other hears loud and clear.

When you're stressed, your brain doesn't keep it to itself. It sends messages all over the body, tightening your shoulders, twisting your stomach, stealing your sleep, and pounding your head like a drum. These are called psychosomatic symptoms, real, physical aches that rise from emotional storms.

Think of it like this: just like too much smoke from the kitchen sets off the fire alarm in the living room, stress in your thoughts sets off sirens in your body. Long-term, this stress becomes like slow poison. It increases inflammation, that sneaky fire that burns quietly in your body and can lead to heart disease, diabetes, even cancer. Not overnight, of course, but drop by drop, like water shaping stone.

But don't worry, my dear. Just like a gentle hand can soothe a crying child, your body responds beautifully when you care for your mind. Yoga, deep breathing, and a good walk in the sun aren't just old-timey remedies, they're science backed ways to tell your nervous system, *"Shhh, you're safe now."* These practices lower cortisol, the stress hormone and bring the body back to balance.

So if your heart is heavy, stretch your body. If your mind is racing, slow your breath. And if your soul is tired, take it outside and let the earth hold you for a while. That's not just healing, that's ancient wisdom meeting modern truth.

Coping Mechanisms and Resilience: Learning to Bend Without Breaking

Life, my dear, will bring storms. There will be hard days, sharp words, silent heartbreaks, and unexpected turns. But how we cope that's what makes all the difference. Coping isn't about pretending nothing's wrong; it's about choosing how we dance in the rain.

There are generally two ways people respond to stress. One is called problem-focused coping, this is when we roll up our sleeves and say, *"Okay, let's fix what's causing this."* Maybe it's setting boundaries, solving a conflict, or making a plan. The other is emotion-focused coping when the situation can't be changed (like grief or uncertainty), so we focus on soothing the heart instead. That might mean journaling, praying, breathing deeply, or just crying in someone's arms.

Now let's talk about resilience, a word that sounds strong, but grows quietly inside us like roots in the earth. Resilience is your bounce-back power your ability to stand again when life has knocked you down. It doesn't mean you never break; it means you learn how to heal smarter each time.

Resilience is built, not born. It grows when we:

- Understand our emotions, rather than burying them.
- Regulate our reactions, so we don't let fear or anger take the wheel.
- Lean on relationships, real ones, where we can be vulnerable.
- Live with purpose, even if it's just knowing *why* we get up in the morning.

Simple daily practices like mindfulness (being fully present), healthy routines (eating, sleeping, moving), and open conversations with safe people become small shields that protect us from being overwhelmed. They don't stop stress from coming, but they help us greet it with steadier hands.

Stress left unchecked will turn into anxiety, but when we face it head on with kindness and clarity, it becomes our guide. Stress points to the parts of our lives begging for attention, discipline, and change. Listen closely, honey, because in stress lies your next lesson.

Pressure doesn't break you, it shapes you. Diamonds don't come from comfort. They come from deep pressure and time. So the next time life gets a little too loud, take a step back, breathe deep, and remember who you are. You come from strong roots, baby. You've got fire in your belly and wisdom in your bones. Stress might visit, but it doesn't get to move in.

Now go on, pour yourself some tea, take a walk, talk to Jesus, or write it out. Whatever you do, don't let stress steal your sparkle. Grandma's watching and she's proud of how far you've come.

Practical Steps to Overcome Stress

(For when you're overwhelmed, under pressure, or just one eye twitch away from a meltdown)

1. Dance in the Bathroom

Yes, seriously. Lock the door. Pick a song that reminds you who the heck you are. Dance like no one's watching (because they aren't). This isn't about looking cool, it's about releasing stuck energy. Move your body and let it shake the stress right out.

2. Box Breathing (4-4-4-4)

Inhale for 4.

Hold for 4.

Exhale for 4.

Hold again for 4.

Repeat 4 times. Instant calm for your nervous system. It's your built-in reset button.

3. The 5-Minute Brain Dump

Grab a notebook (or notes app). Set a timer for 5 minutes. Write every anxious thought, task, and to-do racing through your mind. Don't filter. Just unload. When the timer stops, close it. You've just cleared space in your mental inbox.

4. Walk Like You've Got Somewhere Better to Be

Even if it's just around your house or block. Move with intention. Shoulders back, deep breaths. It helps your body believe you're safe and in control, even if you're faking it at first.

5. Pray, Speak, or Whisper It Out

Talk to Jesus, your grandma, the universe, anyone. Say what's heavy out loud. Healing doesn't always happen in silence. There's power in speaking truth.

6. Make a Cup of Tea Like It's a Ritual

Boil the water. Smell the herbs. Hold the mug with both hands. Sip slowly. Let it ground you in the present moment. This isn't just tea, it's therapy.(if you are a coffee person you know..)

7. Create Something Small

Color a page, write a poem, doodle your stress monster. Creating gives the chaos a form and gives you power back.

8. Digital Detox (Even for 20 Minutes)

Turn off the notifications. Step away from the scrolling. The world can wait.

9. Touch Something Soft

Wrap up in a blanket. Hold a warm mug. Pet your dog. Physical comfort signals to your brain: "I'm okay."

10. Text a Friend: "Can I vent for 2 minutes?"

You don't need advice. You just need a human. Let someone hold your emotions with you, even briefly.

11. Say This Out Loud:

"I am allowed to rest. I am allowed to not have it all figured out. This moment is not the whole story."

Stress can't hold its grip when you meet it with movement, breath, and self-compassion.

Pick two or three from this list when you're spiraling.

Make them your own.

And if all else fails...Bathroom Beyoncé Mode. Always.

"Almost everything will work again if you unplug it for a few minutes, including you." – Anne Lamott

X

Faith – The Art of Trusting Divine Timing

"Faith is taking the first step even when you don't see the whole staircase."-Martin Luther King Jr.

(It's like holdin' out for the man God picked, not the one your loneliness picked off Instagram like it was a clearance sale.)

Now listen here, sugar.

Faith isn't some dusty keepsake you only remember when things go sideways, it's your walking stick. Faith is bold. Faith is gritty. Faith has elbows and a spine. It's not a soft "maybe"; it's a stubborn "yes" in a world full of maybes.

Faith means trusting even when life is messier than your relative's life. It's standing still when everyone's running around like chickens without heads. And sometimes? It's having the nerve to laugh when nothing's funny, because deep down you know God's cooking up something good, even if you ain't got the recipe yet. Let me tell you what I heard from that sharp dressed man Steve Harvey, yes, the one with the mustache fancier than Kangana's airport looks. He said something I won't forget: *"Every prayer you send up is immediately packaged and sent to your address by the Divine, but the delivery date? That's always a surprise."* Now baby, ain't that the truth?

We're so busy pacing the porch, checking the mailbox every five minutes, shaking the gate. And when nothing shows up on *our* schedule, we huff and puff and storm back inside only to find out that our blessing showed up right after we left. You ever missed a delivery because you ran to the store for five minutes? That's what we do with faith. We leave the place God told us to wait, not because we're bad people, just impatient ones. But oh honey, even impatience can be a lesson in disguise. Now don't beat yourself up.

I've stomped off a time or two myself, hair in rollers, mumbling to God. But you know what I realized?Sometimes walking away isn't a lack of faith, it's divine redirection.bGod ain't Amazon. He's not in a rush to deliver what ain't good for you. You want to know how I figured that out? Imagine your baby asking to cuddle a shiny, slithery, glitter-covered snake. Cute? Maybe. Deadly? Absolutely. Now would you let 'em have it? Of course not!

Not because you're mean. Because you've got eyes and a brain and love too deep to be fooled by glitter. That's how God loves us. *"Sometimes what you think you want is just a snake in sequins."*

So when that man you thought was "The One" ghosted you? When the job you were sure was yours slipped away? When the dream you clung to fell apart? Baby, that wasn't punishment. That was protection wearing its tough boots. I used to think faith meant holding on to people, plans, and Pinterest boards. But I ended up losing myself trying to force things that weren't meant for me. Gave away my peace like it was on clearance. And then, your cool Granny had to learn to let go the hard way.

And child... when I did? Peace came rushing in like the Holy Spirit at a tent revival.

Because faith isn't about clinging. It's about releasing. It's not saying, "God, do it my way." It's saying, "Lord, even if You don't, I'll still praise You anyway."

"Let go, and let God."
(And if that doesn't work, take a nap and let Him handle it while you rest.)

Now, faith ain't always comfortable. It requires patience when you'd rather push. Stillness when you want to sprint. It demands that you stay calm when the world's louder. *"Faith is trusting that what didn't happen is just as important as what did."* So when life shuts a door, or slams it, bolts it, and installs a security system don't go trying to crawl through the dog flap. You're not a squirrel. You're a child of God. That closed door just means He's leading you somewhere better.

"Be still, and know that I am God." — Psalm 46:10
(Translation: Sit your ass down and trust Me — I got this.)

I've cried into enough pillows to start my own cotton farm, baby. I've asked, "Why me?" more times than I care to count. But over time, that "why" turned into "what is this teaching me?" And one day, out of the blue I whispered: "Thank You... even for this."

And wouldn't you know that's when peace started blooming like wildflowers.

"Faith is not believing God can, it's knowing He will... in His time, in His way, and for your highest good."

So if you're reading this feeling behind, forgotten, or frustrated, listen to your grandma:

You're not behind. You're right on time. You're not forgotten. You're being refined.

You're not lost. You're being led. Keep showing up. Keep praying. Keep dancing in your kitchen if it helps. But don't you dare try to control it all. Let go, and let faith carry you.

Because in the end, faith isn't about guarantees. It's about trust. It's about peace in the pause.

And it's about becoming the kind of soul who radiates calm, not because life is easy, but because you know God's got hands steady enough to hold it all.

"Those who leave everything in God's hands... will eventually see God's hands in everything."

The Placebo Effect: "Sometimes, Belief is the Best Medicine."

Now baby, listen here, scientists have been scratchin' their heads for years over this thing called the **Placebo Effect**, and it's one of my favorite ways to show how powerful *faith* really is. The idea is simple: if you *believe* a treatment will work even if it's just a sugar pill or plain ol' saltwater your body often starts healing anyway. And no, this ain't just a feel good fairy tale. It's *real science.*

Back in the 1950s, Dr. Henry Beecher, a World War II doctor noticed that soldiers who were given saltwater instead of morphine (because they ran out) still felt pain relief, because they believed it was morphine. Can you imagine that? A little saltwater and a whole lotta belief! That's the body saying, "Well, if she thinks it's medicine, I better get to work."

Fast forward to today, and **clinical trials** across the world still use placebos to test how strong a new drug is, because **in up to 30–60% of cases**, people respond positively to the fake treatment. That's your brain releasing real chemicals like **endorphins and dopamine**, which lower pain, improve mood, and boost healing, just because it believes it's supposed to.

"The placebo effect is the most compelling evidence we have that the mind can heal the body." – Dr. Lissa Rankin

"Belief creates the actual fact." – William James (father of American psychology)

So what's that tell us, sweet pea? That faith isn't just good for the soul, it's got the power to turn the body's light switch on. You think better, and your body feels better. That's divine design right there. I always say: *"If your spirit believes you're gonna make it, your body usually listens."* Heck, sometimes I'd slap a bit of Vicks on my knees, pray over 'em, and wake up feelin' like I'd been to a spa in heaven. It wasn't the rub, child. It was the faith in the fix.

So no, faith ain't foolish. It's the body's *first responder*. Science is just now catchin' up to what Grandma's known for decades, belief is medicine, baby. You've got a whole pharmacy inside of you, and the key to unlockin' it? Is *faith*.

Learned Optimism

Now sit down, baby, and let Grandma tell you somethin' mighty important: you ain't born a grump. You *learn* to be one. And just the same, you can learn to see the sunshine too, even when the sky's grey. That's what this smart fella, **Dr. Martin Seligman**, found in his *Positive Psychology* research. He called it **Learned Optimism**. Fancy name, sweet truth.

He studied how people deal with tough times and found that folks who bounce back the ones who keep on hoping and moving aren't just lucky or naturally cheerful. Nope. They *train* their minds to respond to hardship differently. Instead of saying, *"Why is this always happening to me?"*, they say, *"This is tough, but it won't last forever. I can get through it."* Now that's optimism with muscles.

Dr. Seligman tested this on people, schools, even sports teams, and saw that when folks learned to flip the script on negative thoughts, their depression went down and their performance went up. Faith and optimism, baby, they ain't soft, they're strength in a pretty dress.

"A pessimist sees the difficulty in every opportunity; an optimist sees the opportunity in every difficulty."- Winston Churchill

Now let me tell you something that'll stick to your ribs: **Faith is like optimism that grew a backbone.** It doesn't just hope things will turn out alright , it trusts there's a reason for the mess, even when you're still sittin' in it. It's the quiet voice in your heart sayin', "I don't see the road, but I know it's there. So I'm gonna keep walkin' anyway." Faith and optimism are twins, but faith's the older, wiser sister. She's seen some storms, buried some dreams, and still smiles in the morning. Because she knows: even if today is hard, there's a bigger picture still being painted. And baby, that picture? It's got your joy in it.

The Broaden and Build Theory

Listen, my dear, this smart woman, Dr. Barbara Fredrickson, says that when you feel positive things like hope, love, or faith, it's like your mind stretches wide open, like a big window letting in fresh air. Suddenly, you start seeing new possibilities, you feel stronger, and you connect better with others. That's the magic of faith it's not just wishful thinking, it's opening yourself to all the good that's waiting.

Now, between you and me, at my age, faith is what keeps me going and apparently, it's what caught the eye of a young man I'm seeing! He says I am the most beautiful woman he has seen.*Faith isn't just hope wearing Sunday best, it's steady, strong, and sometimes surprising, like finding a new dance partner when you thought the music had stopped.*

So next time you feel stuck, remember: a little faith ain't just a whisper inside you it's the open door to a bigger, better you. Like Grandma's pie, it's full of sweet surprises, and it's always worth the wait.

Psychoneuroimmunology (PNI)

Faith isn't just for the soul it's like giving your cells a warm hug, and trust me, they love it. Sugarplum listen carefully now. There's this fancy science called **Psychoneuroimmunology**, try saying that five times fast! What it means is this: your thoughts and feelings don't just stay in your head. Oh no! They send messages all the way down to your immune system, the little army inside you that fights off colds, flu, and all sorts of trouble.

Now here's the juicy part, when you believe in something bigger than yourself, when you have faith, your body actually calms down. Stress takes a step back, and suddenly your immune system gets stronger. People with faith tend to get sick less often, and when they do, they bounce back faster. It's not magic, it's science!

As the wise Maya Angelou once said, *"Faith is the bird that feels the light and sings when the dawn is still dark."* Even when life's stormy, faith keeps your inner song going and that makes your body want to keep dancing too.

And you know what? The legendary Norman Cousins, who healed himself from a serious illness by laughing and staying positive, proved this. He believed joy and faith were powerful medicine and guess what? Science agrees. *"Your mind talks to your body more than you think so fill it with faith, and your cells will thank you."* . So, next time you feel worried or tired, remember: your faith isn't just in the sky somewhere. It's inside you, whispering strength to every cell, making you healthier and happier. That's a promise, straight from my heart to yours.

Terror Management Theory (TMT)

"Faith doesn't make the scary things disappear, it just teaches you how to give them a cup of chai and sit with them."

Look, baby, this fancy thing called Terror Management Theory tells us that when we believe in something bigger than ourselves whether that's God, the universe, or just good old hope it helps us handle the biggest fear of all: the fear of not being here anymore. Death, uncertainty, all those heavy thoughts, they come knocking, and faith is the door we open instead of running. Faith doesn't make fear vanish like magic, no. It softens the sting. It gives that fear a meaning, a reason to hang around until you learn from it, not just freak out.

You know, the great Rumi once said, *"Don't grieve. Anything you lose comes round in another form."* Faith tells you suffering and chaos aren't just pain, they're the soil where your strength and peace grow.Fear is a guest that nobody wants, but faith is the cup of tea that makes the waiting bearable.

Grandma's Practical Steps to Grow Your Faith

1. Start small, even a tiny seed grows into a mighty tree.
   Don't wait for big miracles. Begin by trusting the little things: the sun rising, a kind word, a small answered prayer. Faith grows step by step, like watering a plant every day.
2. Read a little every day, not just fancy books, but good words from the heart.
   Pick up scriptures, poems, or inspiring stories. Let those words settle in like warm honey. The mind needs food for faith just like the body needs food for strength.
3. Talk to God like talking to an old friend who's always listening.
   Prayer isn't about perfect words. It's about showing up and sharing worries, hopes, and even grumbles. Faith loves honest conversations.
4. Remember, patience is the slow cooker of faith.
   Faith doesn't rush. It simmers gently while waiting. So when things seem slow or confusing, remind yourself: good things take time.
5. Surround yourself with believers.
   Find friends, family, or communities who lift you up and share their faith stories.
6. Practice letting go, like dropping a heavy basket.
   Faith grows when control loosens. Trust that the God has your back, even

when the plan isn't clear.

7. Keep a faith journal write down little wins and answered prayers. Looking back shows how far faith has carried you. Like an old photo album, full of reminders of love and miracles.

XI

Take It One Day at a Time

"Finish each day and be done with it. You have done what you could."- Ralph Waldo Emerson

Darlin', let Grandma tell you a little secret that most folks spend their whole lives trying to learn: life gets a whole lot simpler and sweeter when you just take it one day at a time. We humans, bless our anxious little hearts, tend to live either in yesterday's regrets or tomorrow's fears. But sugar, the only day you've truly got is today. And that's more than enough.

Most of the time, our unhappiness isn't because life is all that bad, it's because we're living in the wrong time zone. Not in hours or cities, but in our minds. We're worried about next month's bills, next year's career, or next week's conversation that hasn't even happened. We forget that the power is in the present. As the wise Buddha once said, "Do not dwell in the past, do not dream of the future, concentrate the mind on the present moment."

Now honey, let Grandma remind you of something else: most of what you're worried about will never come to pass. That big ol' storm in your head? It's often nothing but clouds of your own imagination. While you're fretting over a future that ain't promised, life is quietly slipping by. And time? Time is a one way street. Once it's gone, there ain't no turning back. That's why you gotta live like you mean it, right here, right now. "Yesterday is gone. Tomorrow has not yet come. We have only today. Let us begin." - Mother Teresa

Take your work, for instance. You don't need to have your whole five-year plan figured out. Just show up today. Give your best. Pour your heart into what's in front of you. Because when you go to bed at night knowing you did your best, there's a peace that no praise or paycheck can give you. Grandma would always say, "Strong discipline earns you quiet confidence and that's the kind that don't shake easy." As Satchel Paige once said, "Work like you don't need the money. Love like you've never been hurt. Dance like nobody's watching."

And oh, sugar, let's talk about love. If there's one thing Grandma learned the hard way, it's that nothing in this world lasts forever, not even the people we love most. That's why you don't let the sun set on anger. Say "I love you" more often. Apologize first. Hug tighter. Don't wait for the perfect moment it might never come. And if tomorrow doesn't show up? Make sure the people you love know they mattered. That's the kind of peace that lets you sleep at night. Gandhi got it right when he said, "Live as if you were to die tomorrow. Learn as if you were to live forever."

That's what taking life one day at a time means. Loving hard. Learning deep. Living fully. There's real wisdom in the old ways, child. Stoic philosophers like Marcus Aurelius used to say, "Confine yourself to the present." And don't that sound like Grandma's advice too? Stop worrying 'bout the future, stop dragging the past around like a ball and chain. Be here. Now.

Psychology calls it "flow," that beautiful state where your mind is wrapped around what you're doing, fully present and alive. Dr. Mihaly Csikszentmihalyi, who studied this stuff like Grandma studies recipes, said it best: "The best moments usually occur if a person's body or mind is stretched to its limits in a voluntary effort to accomplish something difficult and worthwhile." This explains how people achieve peak performance and fulfillment when they are fully engaged in what they are doing, free from distraction or worry. When you give your all to the moment, you enter a state of deep focus where time seems to dissolve, and your actions become effortless yet impactful.

Most of our worries exist only in our minds before they ever take shape in reality. Through a negative belief system, we unconsciously influence events, often manifesting unfavorable outcomes simply by expecting them. Buddhist teachings tell us the same, suffering often comes from attachment to the past or fear of the unknown. So whether it's your health, your dreams, your relationships, or your work, give your 100% today. Not because tomorrow might be hard, but because today is a sacred chance. This day is your gift. And baby, the way you treat it says a whole lot about how you love yourself. Integrity isn't about the spotlight. It's about doing right by yourself even when no one's watching. When you show up every day, even quietly, you build a life of consistency. And consistency, Grandma always said, is just showing up one good day after another. Not all at once. Just today, then tomorrow's today, and so on.

Every great soul who ever lived did it one moment at a time. No shortcuts, no fast-forwards. Just faithful footsteps, steady breath, and a heart rooted in the now. Lewis Carroll once said, "In the end, we only regret the chances we didn't take, the relationships we were afraid to have, and the decisions we waited too long to make." Baby, when you give your all to this day, to your mental health, physical health, your dreams and your people, you build self-respect, discipline, and a deep sense of peace. That kind of peace don't come from how much you've achieved, but from knowing you lived today fully, wholly, and honestly.

The Science Behind Taking Life One Day at a Time

Now baby, if you think Grandma's just spinning sweet nothings about "one day at a time," let me tell you science backs this up.

Mindfulness: The Power of Present Awareness

Mindfulness is all about fully paying attention to the present moment without judgment or distraction. When you focus on "now" rather than worrying about what's past or future, your mind calms down. Scientific studies, especially those on Mindfulness-Based Stress Reduction (MBSR), show that practicing mindfulness lowers anxiety, improves emotional regulation, and boosts overall well being. It's like giving your busy brain a gentle hug and telling it, "It's okay, just this moment is enough."

How the Brain Handles Stress

Our brains are wired to keep us safe by reacting to threats, real or imagined. The prefrontal cortex, the part responsible for planning and decision making, gets overwhelmed when flooded with stress hormones like cortisol. Constant worry about tomorrow or regret over yesterday keeps your stress levels high, harming memory, mood, and even sleep. By focusing on today, you reduce this flood of stress chemicals, giving your brain and body a chance to heal and rest.

Locus of Control: Owning Your Power

Psychologists talk about something called the locus of control, whether you believe you control your life (internal) or that outside forces decide for you (external). People who take it one day at a time tend to have an internal locus of control. They focus on what they *can* do right now, which builds resilience and confidence. This mindset shift moves you from feeling powerless to feeling like the captain of your own ship, steering through calm and storm alike.

Cognitive Behavioral Therapy (CBT) and Breaking Down Worries

CBT is a common therapeutic approach that helps people manage anxiety by breaking big, overwhelming problems into smaller, manageable steps. Therapists often encourage grounding yourself in what's happening *today* as a way to reduce anxiety about the future. This "one day at a time" approach helps interrupt the cycle of negative thinking and makes problems feel less daunting, exactly like Grandma's advice to focus on the now.

Ancient Wisdom Across Cultures

Buddhist teachings urge us to release attachment to past pain and future fear. The Stoics, like Marcus Aurelius, emphasized focusing only on what's within your control here and now. Even Christian prayers ask for "daily bread," and not the months or the years symbolizing the sacredness of daily sustenance. Across religions and philosophies, the present moment is honored as the only true reality we can fully embrace.

Practical Steps to Practice Mindfulness

1. Start with Your Breath

Darlin', your breath is always with you, no matter where you are. Begin by simply paying attention to your breathing. Take a slow, deep breath in through your nose, hold it a second, then let it out gently through your mouth. Do this a few times. Notice how your chest rises and falls. This simple act brings your mind back to the present, like a gentle anchor in a busy sea.

2. Notice the Little Things

Grandma says, slow down and really see the world around you. Feel the warmth of the sun on your skin, listen to the birds sing, or savor the taste of your morning tea. These small moments, when noticed fully, bring you into the now and make life richer.

3. Use Your Senses

Pause and tune into your five senses, what do you hear, see, smell, taste, and touch right now? For example, if you're washing dishes, notice the sound of the water, the smoothness of the plates, and the scent of the soap. Engaging your senses helps pull your mind away from

worries and into the present moment.

4. Practice a Body Scan

Take a few minutes to mentally scan your body from head to toe. Notice any areas of tension or discomfort without trying to fix them, just observe. This helps you become aware of how stress shows up in your body and gives you a chance to relax those muscles, calming your nervous system.

5. Use Mindful Reminders

Grandma says, life gets busy, so set gentle reminders for yourself. This could be a sticky note on your mirror, a chime on your phone, or a bracelet you touch when you remember. Each time you see or hear the reminder, pause for a moment and take a mindful breath.

6. Practice Loving Kindness Meditation

Spend a few minutes silently repeating kind phrases to yourself, like "May I be safe, may I be happy, may I be healthy." Then, expand that kindness to others, friends, family, even those you find challenging. This practice softens your heart and anchors you in compassion and the present moment.

Darling, consistency is one day every day it often looks like a long journey, but it's not. It's just living today, today. So take a deep breath. Breathe in the now. Don't rush through your day like it's a chore. Show up with intention. Sit in the sun a little longer. Taste your tea. Say something kind. Let the moment wrap around you like Grandma's quilt, warm, comforting, and with love. Don't borrow trouble from tomorrow. Bake today's bread, say today's prayers, give today's hugs. That's how you build a life worth remembering.

XII

The Mirage of Satisfaction – The Art of Being Content

"Satisfaction lies in the effort, not in the attainment. Full effort is full victory." –
Mahatma Gandhi

We live in a world that sings the anthem of "more." From the moment you open your eyes to a buzzing screen or a noisy mind, you're nudged, sometimes shoved into the race of desire. More money. More validation. More followers. More recognition. And in that constant chase, we've mistaken movement for meaning. We've confused motion with fulfillment. But here's what no one tells you in the glamour of the goal: satisfaction is a mirage. Yes, darling, it's like the shimmer you see on a long, hot road. You keep driving, thinking it's water, thinking you're almost there but it slips further away. Again. And again.

The Illusion We Chase

I used to think satisfaction would come dressed as applause, a fancy job title, or a moment in a foreign land where I could post a picture and say, "I've made it." But every single time I got there, I felt hollow. Like someone who had finally climbed a ladder only to realize it was leaning against the wrong wall. It's not that ambition is bad. No, child. Dream big. But don't let those dreams rob you of the miracle of now. Because this very moment, the tea in your hand, the breath in your lungs, the smile of someone who loves you that is where contentment hides.

You see, what you hold right now, someone else is praying for. And you? You're too busy eyeing the next thing to notice.

"Gratitude turns what we have into enough." – Aesop

Why We Keep Running

Science gives us an answer too. Our brains are wired for pursuit. Dopamine, the neurotransmitter of desire, spikes not when we get something, but when we're about to. That's why the chase feels better than the catch. But here's where wisdom must meet biology: if you never learn to pause, to appreciate the moment you once prayed for, you'll spend your entire life running in circles, collecting trophies that collect dust in your soul. Even if you land on the moon, you'll return asking, "Now what?" Because the problem is not the moon, it's the belief that arrival will finally quiet the longing.

"You can never get enough of what you don't really need."- Eric Hoffer

Contentment Isn't Passive, It's Powerful

Let me tell you something, child. Contentment isn't about giving up. It's not laziness. It's not apathy. It's the power of looking life in the eye and saying, "I have enough. I am enough." That's not weakness. That's strength. That's freedom. The Bible says, *"I have learned to be content whatever the circumstances."* (Philippians 4:11). It doesn't say contentment comes naturally. No, you learn it. You practice it. Like kneading dough or tending to a garden. And some days, you'll forget. That's alright. Just come back home to gratitude.

The Downhill Ride

Imagine climbing a hill on a bicycle, gearless, on a hot summer day. Your legs ache. Your lungs burn. You're tempted to give up. But you keep pushing. And when you finally reach the top and begin to coast, the breeze hits your face like grace. That, my love, is contentment. Not the destination, but the relief of having endured and chosen to feel the reward of now. That's the art. Not just getting there. But allowing yourself to feel the beauty of it.

"Happiness is not something you postpone for the future; it is something you design for the present."-Jim Rohn

The Quiet Abundance

There's a quiet kind of abundance that doesn't post itself online. It's found in slow mornings, deep conversations, belly laughs, clean bedsheets, prayers answered in silence, and knowing you did your best even if no one clapped.That's the kind of life worth living. Not loud, but full. Not flashy, but grounded.

Because sometimes, peace isn't in the next peak, but in sitting under your own tree, sipping your own tea, and realizing: *this is enough.* And if Grandma could whisper in your ear right now, she'd say, "Baby, if you don't learn to find joy in the ordinary, the extraordinary will always feel empty."

The Dopamine Chase – Why You Keep Reaching for "What's Next," Sweetheart

Now listen here, baby, your brain's a funny little thing. It don't get excited when you *get* the cookie, it gets excited when you *think* about the cookie. You see what I'm sayin'? It's not the having, it's the chasing that gives you that little spark. That spark is called *dopamine*, it's your brain's way of dangling a carrot and saying, "Run, child, run!"

Every time you dream about that new job, that new dress, that new "like" on the internet... your brain lights up like a Christmas tree. But when you *actually* get it? Well, the lights dim. That's why it don't feel as good as you thought it would. And before you can even enjoy what's in your hands, your mind's already on the next shiny thing.

"The wanting brain and the liking brain are not the same," says some big-brained fella named Dr. Kent Berridge. And oh, baby, he's right. So what happens? You keep running. You run from one goal to the next, from one applause to another, from one high to the next like a squirrel on espresso. But darling, that ain't peace, that's exhaustion dressed in ambition.

You ain't tired 'cause you're doing too much work, you're tired 'cause you never stop chasing. Sometimes the most grown-up thing you can do is sit still and say, *"This is enough for today."*

Don't let your life be one long blur of "next." Find a little joy in "now," sugar. The world will keep spinning whether you chase it or not.

The Hedonic Treadmill – Why That Happy Don't Last Long, Sugar

Now listen close, baby, 'cause Grandma's got something important to tell you. You know that big feeling you get when something wonderful happens, like landing your dream job, buying that shiny new car, or falling head-over-heels in love? It's sweet, ain't it? Feels like you could float right up to the heavens.

But here's the kicker: give it a few months, sometimes even just a few weeks and that shiny starts to fade. The job becomes routine, the car gets a scratch, and even that handsome fella leaves the toilet seat up. You go right back to the same old level of happy you had before. That, sweetheart, is what those clever psychologists call the Hedonic Treadmill.

"People are unhappy not because they don't have enough, but because they always want more."

That's the whole idea, from Brickman & Campbell, 1971.

Let me break it down for you : it's like being on one of those treadmills at the gym. You're running, huffin' and puffin', thinkin' you're getting somewhere, but honey, you're still in the same room. No matter how fast you go, your feet don't touch new ground. That's what happens when you keep chasing happiness through stuff, applause, and the next big thing. You think *one more* will do it. One more promotion, one more vacation, one more "look at me" on the internet. But after each "more," you come right back to where you started. Worn out. A little emptier.

"Happiness is not having what you want, but wanting what you have."- Rabbi Hyman Schachtel

You see, child, joy that lasts don't come from *new things*. It comes from *noticing the old ones*. That morning cup of chai, a roof over your head, your mama's voice on the phone, the way the breeze hits your skin when you finally sit down to breathe. That's real wealth. Stillness now *that's* what breaks the cycle. When you stop sprinting for a moment and just say," *This is enough. I am enough."*

That's when you step off the treadmill and start walking on solid ground again.

So next time you feel that itch for more, don't run faster. Just pause, look around, and remember: joy doesn't run. It rests.

Running Toward Joy or Away from Stillness?

Not every chase is noble, and not every longing is honest.

We often tell ourselves that we're chasing dreams, that our hunger for more is a sign of ambition, vision, or drive. But if we peel back the layers, we must ask: **Is this longing really coming from inspiration, or is it born from insecurity?** Are we genuinely pulled toward joy, or are we quietly pushing ourselves away from the discomfort of stillness?

Stillness is not easy. It demands that we stop distracting ourselves and sit face-to-face with who we are without the noise, without titles, likes, applause, or a calendar full of things that make us feel important. Sometimes, the race we're running isn't toward something greater, it's a sprint away from the ache of not feeling "enough."

"It is not the man who has too little, but the man who craves more, that is poor." – Seneca

We scroll endlessly, set bigger goals, take on more, hoping the next thing will fix the hollow space inside us. But here's the truth You don't need more to be more. You just need to learn how to sit with what you already have, and see it rightly. Stillness reveals what noise hides. When you sit with yourself long enough, you start to hear the quiet truth: You are not behind. You are becoming.

"Almost everything will work again if you unplug it for a few minutes, including you." – Anne Lamott

Yet our minds are conditioned to equate motion with meaning. We think, "If I'm not chasing something, I'm wasting time." But motion without direction is just restlessness wearing sneakers.

What if joy isn't in the running but in the resting well? What if the very thing we've been trying to run away from, silence, solitude, stillness is the only place we can ever truly find contentment?

"There is a time for everything, and a season for every activity under the heavens." – Ecclesiastes 3:1

Even Jesus withdrew from the crowds to be alone in prayer. Even the earth rests between harvests. You don't need to earn rest with achievement. You don't need to prove your worth through exhaustion What if, today, instead of chasing the next milestone, you simply whispered to your soul: "You are safe. You are seen. You are already enough." Because you are.

And when you learn to sit in stillness, you stop running from yourself, and finally start arriving.

Grandma's Guide to Practicing Satisfaction Every Day

1. Wake Up and Give Thanks, Honey

Before you even get outta that bed, thank the Good Lord for another day. Even if the day looks tough, there's always something, breath in your lungs, a roof over your head, a friend's smile that's worth a little gratitude. Grandma says, "Start your day counting blessings, not problems."

2. Taste Your Food Slowly, Sweetheart

Don't just shove it in. Taste it. Enjoy it. Notice the flavors, the warmth, the care that went into it. When you savor the little things, life starts feeling richer. Like my Grandma used to say, "Even a plain dosai tastes better when you chew with love."

3. Stop and Breathe Between Tasks

Don't rush through your day like a runaway train. Pause, take a deep breath, and feel where you are right now. Remember, "The flower don't hurry, but it still blooms." Let yourself bloom slow and steady.

4. Find One Good Thing in the Hard Stuff

Had a tough day? Grandma says, "Look for the silver lining, even if it's just a tiny thread." Maybe you learned something, or got closer to someone, or just survived. Celebrate that small win.

5. Put Down Your Phone and Look Around

Notice the sky, the trees, the people you love. The world is full of beauty that's easy to miss when you're glued to a screen. "Eyes wide open, baby. Life's too short to miss the good parts."

6. Speak Kindly to Yourself

Your words to yourself matter as much as words to others. Treat yourself like you're your own best friend. So say, "I'm doing enough," "I'm worthy," "This moment is good."

7. End Your Day with Quiet Reflection

Before sleep, think about three things that went well today. Even if they're small, like a warm cup of tea or a smile from a stranger. This little habit rewires your brain to notice goodness.

The true treasure isn't found at the finish line, it's in the footsteps you're taking right now. Each moment, each breath, holds the quiet gift of presence . When you shift your focus from chasing what's next to cherishing what is, life unfolds in a way that no ambition ever could. Remember the wisdom from ages past and faith alike:

"Do not worry about tomorrow, for tomorrow will worry about itself. Each day has enough trouble of its own."- Matthew 6:34

Instead of burdening yourself with tomorrow's worries, pour your energy into this very moment, feel it, breathe it, live it fully. Happiness doesn't come wrapped in trophies or new achievements; it blooms from your own actions of gratitude, love, and acceptance. So, let your new quest be a gentle one, not a sprint toward endless desires, but a slow dance with contentment. Not a loud call for more applause, but a quiet celebration of awareness. Not a restless hunt for the next thing, but a heartfelt embrace of the now thing.

"He who is not contented with what he has, would not be contented with what he would like to have."- Socrates

XIII

Love Yourself Enough – The Science, The Spirit, The Stand

"When you know who you are, no one can make you feel small."

There comes a time, yes, even for the tender-hearted, people-pleasing, hopeful you when you have to stop sitting by the emotional window, waiting for someone to love you the way you crave. And instead? Start loving yourself louder. Fiercer. Truer.

Love yourself enough to say **no** without explaining. Enough to draw boundaries not with barbed wire, but with gentle strength. Enough to walk away even if your voice shakes and your heart's still attached. And love yourself enough to protect your peace like your *soul depends on it* because sugar, it absolutely does.

You see, as Grandma would say, *"You can't pour tea for everyone else while your own cup's dry, sweetheart."* So stop begging for crumbs when you were born to feast. The kind of love you want? Start giving it to the mirror. Start building it from the inside out. Because the moment you stop waiting and start choosing yourself that's when the magic begins.

And don't you ever forget: the right love won't make you shrink, chase, or ache. It'll feel like home baby.

The Psychology of Self-Love: More Than a Trend

Self-love is not indulgence. It's not selfishness. It's **psychological hygiene**.

Maslow's hierarchy of needs

Maslow's Hierarchy of Needs

In **Maslow's Hierarchy of Needs**, self-actualization, the peak of human potential can't happen unless foundational needs like self-esteem and belonging are fulfilled. And *you* are responsible for fulfilling your emotional needs first. Waiting for others to give you what you can't give yourself only leads to a cycle of emptiness.

Dr. Kristin Neff, a pioneer in the field of self-compassion, states: "With self-compassion, we give ourselves the same kindness and care we'd give to a good friend." It sounds simple. But how often do you *deny* yourself that kindness? How often do you tell yourself you're not enough?

Psychologist Daniel Goleman, in his groundbreaking work on emotional intelligence, identifies self-awareness as the cornerstone of personal growth. Without it, we are vulnerable to being shaped by external definitions, by what others expect, demand, or assume about us.

When you lack self-awareness, every comment, criticism, or rejection becomes a mirror. You begin to question yourself. You adopt identities that are not yours. And in the process, **you become a distorted version of yourself** smaller, quieter, more fearful.

But when you are self-aware, you become unshakeable. You can observe your emotions, your triggers, your values, and your limits. You can say, "This is not for me," without guilt. You can walk away without explanation. You can choose yourself even when no one else does.

"Until you make the unconscious conscious, it will direct your life and you will call it fate."- Carl Jung

Self-Awareness: The Mirror You Cannot Escape

According to psychologist Daniel Goleman, **self-awareness is the cornerstone of emotional intelligence**. Without it, we're puppets to people's opinions, reactions, and validations. With it, we become authors of our identity.

"Knowing yourself is the beginning of all wisdom." – Aristotle

Without self-awareness, people define you. Their opinions become your mirror. You begin to believe the lies: *You're too much. You're not enough. You're replaceable. You're weak.*

But when you're aware of who you are, those opinions become *background noise.* You no longer chase people to feel seen. Because you already *see yourself,* clearly and wholly.

The Cost of Ignoring Your Boundaries

Here's a truth rooted in neuroscience: chronic people pleasing rewires your brain to associate acceptance with self betrayal. Every time you say "yes" when your heart says "no," you reinforce a neurological pattern that equates love with pain, and connection with discomfort. This is not just emotional damage, it's neurological self-sabotage. You are not required to set yourself on fire to keep others warm. Every unnecessary "yes" is a betrayal of your inner voice. Every time you stay silent when your soul wants to speak, you weaken the relationship you have with yourself. Over time, this creates internal conflict: You no longer feel at peace because you are no longer in alignment.

When You Don't Say No

You start betraying yourself in small ways.

You go to dinners you hate.

Laugh at jokes that hurt.

Agree to things that drain you.

Stay silent when your soul is screaming.

And little by little, you begin to disappear.

You become a stranger to your own reflection.

In behavioral psychology, this is known as **cognitive dissonance**, the discomfort that arises when your actions contradict your values. It is not just emotional; it affects your mental clarity, self esteem, and even physical health. Chronic stress, anxiety, and depression often stem from years of being who we are not. This isn't just emotional it's *chemical*. People pleasing trains your brain to associate approval with pain. That's not survival. That's trauma. And it's okay to call it that.

But you don't have to keep living there. Say no. Often. Loudly. Kindly. But firmly.
It is not your job to manage how others feel about your truth. It's your job to protect your soul.

Boundaries: The Silent Language of Self-Respect

Boundaries are not walls; they are gates. They don't shut people out, they teach them how to *enter your life respectfully*. According to **Attachment Theory**, people with secure boundaries tend to form healthier relationships, experience less anxiety, and are better equipped to handle conflict. This is *emotional maturity*. Let this sink in: If you don't set your boundaries, someone else will set your limits.

Healing the Inner Child: The Root of Self-Neglect

Much of our inability to love ourselves stems from wounds we never asked for. If you grew up constantly seeking approval, you probably learned that your worth was tied to performance, perfection, or pleasing others. But you're not that child anymore. You get to *re-parent* yourself now. You get to say:

- "I am enough even when I'm not needed."
- "I am loved even when I say no."
- "I am safe even when I disappoint someone."

"You have been criticizing yourself for years, and it hasn't worked. Try approving of yourself and see what happens." – Louise Hay

Your Light Doesn't Have to Dim for Others to Shine

When you truly love yourself, you don't fear others' success, beauty, or strength. You *honor* it. Because you know their light doesn't dim yours it adds to it. But you must *guard* that light. People will try to shrink you to fit their comfort. They'll hand you watered down versions of yourself to drink and call it humility. Don't accept it.

You can be humble and powerful.
You can be gentle and firm.
You can be kind and commanding.

Your authenticity is not up for compromise.

"You alone are enough. You have nothing to prove to anybody." – Maya Angelou

"Don't shrink yourself to fit places you've outgrown." – Unknown

"When you say 'yes' to others, make sure you are not saying 'no' to yourself." – Paulo Coelho

Practical Reflections & Tools:

1. Journal Prompts

- Where in my life am I betraying myself for the comfort of others?
- What is one boundary I know I need to set today?
- What limiting belief about myself am I ready to release?

2. Affirmations for Self-Love & Awareness

- I am safe to be seen in my fullness.
- I am not defined by others' opinions of me.
- My 'no' is powerful. My 'yes' is sacred.
- I am whole. I am worthy. I am enough.

3. Daily Practice

- 10 minutes of mindfulness: Breathe and check in with your emotions. Ask, *what do I need today?*
- Mirror Talk: Look at yourself in the mirror and say one kind thing out loud.
- One 'No' per day: Practice saying no in small ways to build self-trust.

Honey, loving yourself enough means never letting anyone write your story with words you wouldn't choose for yourself. It means standing up for your soul, even when your voice shakes. It means walking away when you know staying would destroy your peace. It means knowing you're already whole, even with your scars. At the end of the day, you are all you've got. And that's not a limitation, it's your superpower. So love yourself.

Loudly. Radically. Fearlessly.

Enough.

XIV

Embrace Your Flaws – The Radical Art of Being Perfectly Imperfect

"There is a crack in everything. That's how the light gets in." - Leonard Cohen

Listen up, darlings, your grandma's about to drop some truth bombs that'll make you see your "flaws" in a whole new light. We live in a world obsessed with filters, fillers, and faking it, but here's the real tea: perfection is a myth, and chasing it will only make you miserable.

The Universal Truth: Everyone's Got Something

Let's get real for a second:

- Marilyn Monroe's iconic beauty mark? Considered a "flaw" by old school Hollywood standards until she made it her signature.

Marilyn Monroe's iconic beauty mark

- Steve Jobs' temper? The same intensity that made him difficult also built Apple.
- Michelangelo's David? The statue has a slightly crooked nose and asymmetrical eyes, and it's still considered one of the most perfect artworks ever created.

Michelangelo's David

"Perfection is not attainable, but if we chase perfection we can catch excellence." - Vince Lombardi

The Science of Imperfection

Your brain is wired to notice your own flaws 10x more than others do . Here's what research tells us:

- The "Spotlight Effect": You think everyone notices your flaws as much as you do. Truth, they don't. (Harvard study proved we overestimate scrutiny by 40%)
- Japanese Kintsugi: The 15th century art of repairing broken pottery with gold teaches us that breaks make something more valuable.

Kintsugi

Psychology Today reports that people who embrace their perceived flaws show 23% higher resilience in facing life's challenges.

Flaws That Made History

Some of humanity's greatest breakthroughs came from what others called "imperfections":

- Albert Einstein was labeled "slow" by his teachers. His unconventional thinking rewrote physics.

- Richard Branson's dyslexia made traditional schooling difficult, so he built a billion dollar empire instead.

"I am careful not to confuse excellence with perfection. Excellence I can reach for; perfection is God's business." - Michael J. Fox

Prescription for Flawed Living

1. The Mirror Challenge: Every morning, point out one "flaw" and reframe it as a strength. ("My vulnerability" = "My kindness")
2. Collect Imperfect Icons: Make a list of successful people who turned their "flaws" into superpowers.
3. Practice Wabi-Sabi: The Japanese philosophy of finding beauty in imperfection. That coffee stain on your shirt? Character.

Example of Wabi-Sabi

Your quirks aren't mistakes, they're your fingerprint on the world. That thing you've spent years hiding? It might be exactly what makes you unforgettable. *"You are imperfect, permanently and inevitably flawed. And you are beautiful."* — Amy Bloom

Now go forth and be gloriously, unapologetically imperfect. After all, as this grandma always says: "Life's too short to waste on being someone else's version of perfect."

My Personal Battle with Flaws: A Story of Skin, Scars, and Self-Rediscovery

"We don't see things as they are, we see them as we are." - Anaïs Nin

Let me tell you a story, sweetheart, one about mirrors, masks, and finally finding the courage to take them off. For four long years, I waged war against my own reflection. Not just against acne, but against the shame it carried. And honey, let me tell you, it was never really about skin.

The Prison I Built Myself

Those well-meaning voices *"Just wash your face more!"* *"Try cutting dairy!"*, pierced like backhanded hugs. The truth? No turmeric mask could heal what really hurt:

- The imagined stares burning hotter than benzoyl peroxide
- The concealer rituals even to take out the trash
- The midnight prayers bargaining with God for new skin like it was my soul that needed replacing

"I didn't just have acne, I became acne."
Research shows what I learned the hard way:

- 85% of people with acne report lowered self-esteem (Journal of Clinical & Aesthetic Dermatology)
- The brain processes social rejection like physical pain (Harvard Neuroscience)
- We overestimate how much others notice our flaws by 40% (Cornell's Spotlight Effect Study)

The Moment Everything Changed

Then came the words that shattered my prison:
"Darling, people aren't studying you, they're terrified you're studying them."
Suddenly, I remembered:

- My favorite teacher had crooked teeth and gave the best advice
- The friend who comforted me had scars she never explained

- The love of my life still talks about how I *laughed*, not how I looked

"We remember people's humanity long after we forget their imperfections."
The Liberating Truth
Here's what acne (and every flaw) tries to convince you:

1. It's all people see (False—most don't notice)
2. It defines your worth (Dangerous lie)
3. You're alone in this (The most vicious untruth of all)

Science backs up the wisdom:

- Self-compassion reduces shame faster than perfectionism (Dr. Kristin Neff, UT Austin)
- Vulnerability strengthens connections (Brené Brown's 7-year research)
- Your brain's neuroplasticity means you can rewrite your self-story at any time

The Alchemy of Acceptance
The journey wasn't about clear skin, it was about:
Transferring power from my flaws to my freedom
Replacing "What's wrong with me?" with "What's strong in me?"
Understanding that confidence isn't the absence of insecurity, it's the courage to exist fully anyway

A Letter to My Younger Self
"Dear girl hiding in bathroom stalls reapplying makeup:
One day, you'll walk barefaced into a room and light it up with your laugh.
Your 'flaws' will become the compass that leads others home to themselves.
The cracks you hate? They'll be where your wisdom seeps through.
Keep going."

Now it is Your Turn
Whatever your "acne" is, your body, your past, your quirks, hear this:

- The things you think disqualify you are preparing you
- Every great person in history carried scars (visible or not)
- Healing begins when you stop hiding

"When we deny our stories, they define us. When we own our stories, we get to write the ending." - Brené Brown

Now go look in the mirror and say it with your whole chest: *"This is my face. This is my story. And I choose to wear both with pride."*

After all, darling the world doesn't need you to be perfect. It needs you to be present. And that starts with showing up as you are.

Guide to Flaw Flirting (Daily Steps That Actually Work)

1. The "Flaw Audit" (Morning Ritual)

"Darling, name it to tame it."

- Do this: While brushing your teeth, point at one "flaw" in the mirror and say:
  "Okay, [crooked nose/acne/quirky laugh], you're part of the team now. Let's make today great anyway."
- Why it works: A UCLA study found naming emotions reduces their power, same goes for flaws.

2. The "5-Second Rule" (For Comparison Traps)

"Sweetheart, social media is a highlight reel don't compare your behind-the-scenes to someone else's fireworks."

- Do this: When you catch yourself comparing, snap your fingers 5 times and say:
  "Their journey isn't mine. My story's still being written."

3. The "Wabi-Sabi Pause" (Mindfulness Hack)

"Japanese art fixes broken pottery with gold, baby. Be your own kintsugi."

- Do this: At lunch, examine an "imperfect" object (chipped mug, wrinkled napkin). Say:
  "You're still useful. Just like me."
- Science says: Practicing radical acceptance lowers cortisol by 23% (Journal of Behavioral Therapy).

4. The "Flaw-Flipping" Journal Prompt (Nightly)

"Turn your 'weaknesses' into secret weapons, honey."

- Do this: Before bed, write:
"Today, my [flaw] actually helped me by __________."
(Example: *"My loud laugh made a stranger smile."*)

5. The "Vulnerability Dare" (Weekly Challenge)
"Confidence isn't 'they won't notice', it's 'I don't care if they do.'"

- Do this: Once a week, intentionally expose a flaw:

  - Go makeup-free to the grocery store
  - Say *"I don't know"* in a meeting
  - Post an unedited photo

- Why: A Harvard study found vulnerability increases likability by 37%.

6. The "Ancestor Alignment" (Perspective Shift)
"Darling, your 'flaws' are someone's survival story."

- Do this: Pick a physical trait you dislike. Research its ethnic/evolutionary purpose:

  - Curly hair? Traps moisture in hot climates.(We all know that is like the dream so its okay to use that as an example)

- Say: *"This isn't a flaw, it's my heritage in HD."*

"You are imperfect, permanently and inevitably flawed. And you are beautiful." – Amy Bloom

The goal is not to fix every flaw. The goal is to live fully, love deeply, and shine **with** the flaws, not in spite of them. Because often, it is your *cracks* that let your *light* shine through. So baby go ahead embrace your flaws. They are the map of your becoming.

XV
Treat Your Body Like a Temple

"You don't have a soul. You are a soul. You have a body." - C.S. Lewis

Let that sink in baby. You, the thinker, the dreamer, the believer, you exist inside a body. And this body, this incredible, miraculous machine, is the only one you will ever have. How you treat it reflects how much you value yourself. It is not just a vessel; it is a sacred home for your soul, your energy, your purpose.

And yet, too often we neglect this temple. We overfeed it, under-nourish it, push it to exhaustion, or ignore its cries for movement and rest. We wait until illness strikes before we pause. But the truth is: you can't pour from an empty cup. You can't build a peaceful life in a chaotic body.

Your Body Reflects Your Inner World

"The body is the mirror of the mind. It reflects our thoughts, beliefs, and emotional state." - Louise Hay

Baby, science has now proven what ancient cultures always believed, your physical health and mental state are interconnected. The gut, for example, is now known as the "second brain." It contains over 100 million neurons and is directly connected to your brain via the vagus nerve. When you eat unhealthy food, it not only harms your digestion, but also affects your mood, memory, and focus.

- Poor diet = low energy, brain fog, and anxiety.
- Healthy diet = mental clarity, emotional balance, and joy.

If you constantly feed your body with sugar, processed foods, and unhealthy fats, your cells become inflamed. Inflammation is now linked to depression, mood disorders, and fatigue. What you eat literally becomes your thoughts.

The Deadly Sins of Gluttony & Sloth: Modern Epidemics

Historically, gluttony (overindulgence in food) and sloth (laziness) were considered spiritual weaknesses. Today, they are normalized through fast food culture, binge eating media, and the glorification of "foodie" lifestyles.

Let's break it down:

- Gluttony: Consuming more than needed. Overeating slows down your metabolism, increases insulin resistance, and leads to obesity, diabetes, and heart disease.
- Sloth: A direct consequence of poor eating. Junk food causes blood sugar crashes that make you tired, cranky, and demotivated. This leads to inactivity, which worsens both physical and mental health.

According to the World Health Organization:

- Depression is now the leading cause of disability worldwide- and unhealthy lifestyle is a major contributor.

These statistics are not just numbers, they're a wake-up call.

Fasting: Ancient Wisdom, Modern Science

"Fasting is not just a physical discipline; it is a spiritual feast." - Jentezen Franklin

Fasting is one of the oldest healing traditions in human history. From Greek philosophers like Hippocrates, who prescribed fasting as medicine, to Prophet Muhammad (PBUH) and Jesus Christ, who both practiced regular fasting, the act of abstaining from food has always been a way to purify the body and align the soul.

Today, science supports what our ancestors knew intuitively. Fasting:

- Boosts autophagy (cellular cleansing process)
- Improves insulin sensitivity (prevents diabetes)
- Enhances brain function (promotes BDNF, the "brain fertilizer")
- Reduces inflammation
- Supports weight loss

- Increases human growth hormone (important for fat burning and muscle gain)

The most popular and science-backed methods:

- Intermittent fasting (16:8): Fast for 16 hours, eat in an 8-hour window.
- 24-hour fasts: Once a week for deep detox.
- Water fasts (36-72 hours) under supervision for advanced cleansing.

My practice: I fast once a week for 24 hours. The physical benefits are evident, better digestion, more energy, clearer skin. But the mental clarity and self-mastery it brings are what I value most. Fasting builds discipline. It teaches me that I control my body, my cravings, and my choices, not the other way around.

Movement is a Form of Worship

"Physical fitness is not only one of the most important keys to a healthy body, it is the basis of dynamic and creative intellectual activity." - John F. Kennedy

Your body was made to move. Exercise doesn't just sculpt muscle,it releases stored trauma, improves hormone balance, and clears emotional stagnation.

- When you move, you release endorphins, the "feel-good" chemicals.
- Exercise increases serotonin and dopamine , the happiness hormones.
- It also lowers cortisol, the stress hormone.

The gym is not a punishment ground. It's a playground for self-respect. Think of your workouts as daily rituals , physical prayers to honor the life within you.

Practical Training Tips:

- Train 4-5 days a week: Include strength, cardio, and flexibility.
- Use compound movements: Squats, deadlifts, push-ups, etc.
- Rest and recover: Muscles grow in rest, not in stress.
- Track progress: Strength, energy levels, mood – all count.

I personally prefer playing some Tamil music and dance my heart out . It makes me so happy.

Eat Like You Love Yourself

"If you keep good food in your fridge, you will eat good food." - Errick McAdams

Your plate is your power. Every meal is a chance to nourish or numb yourself. Eating is not just about taste; it's about intention.

Modern science and ancient wisdom agree: whole, unprocessed foods are the key to vitality.

Healthy Eating Habits (Backed by Science):

- Eat the rainbow: Variety of colorful fruits and vegetables for antioxidants.
- Balance your macros: Carbs, fats, and protein in each meal.
- Limit sugar and seed oils: Linked to inflammation and disease.
- Stay hydrated: Your brain is 75% water. Dehydration causes fatigue.
- Don't eat late at night: Your digestion slows after sunset.
- Practice mindful eating: Chew slowly. Avoid screens. Savor the meal.

Reject "Foodie" Culture - Choose Conscious Eating

The rise of "foodie" culture, food reels, and mukbang videos have normalized overconsumption and emotional eating. We laugh while watching people binge on 10,000 calories, ignoring that this is self-harm disguised as entertainment.

You are not a garbage bin. Your body is sacred.

Conscious eating is the opposite. It's about:

- Asking: "Why am I eating this?"
- Eating when you're hungry, not bored.
- Choosing food that aligns with your goals.
- Being grateful for every bite.

The Mind-Body-Spirit Loop

"A healthy outside starts from the inside." - Robert Urich

Your body is deeply tied to your mental health and spiritual connection.

- When you eat right, you think clearer.
- When you move daily, you feel stronger emotionally.
- When you fast, you reset your desires and reconnect with your deeper self.

This loop feeds itself: a healthy body supports a peaceful mind, which allows spiritual alignment,which in turn inspires better choices for the body. It's all connected.

Worship with Discipline

"Discipline is the highest form of self-love."

Treating your body like a temple isn't about looking perfect. It's about living in harmony with the body that houses your soul. It's about saying: I love myself enough to nourish, protect, and strengthen the only place I truly live.

- Fast weekly to reset and master yourself.
- Move daily to honor the strength within.
- Eat consciously to fuel, not numb.

In a world trying to sell you shortcuts and stimulants, become someone who chooses consistency over chaos. Your body is your altar. Worship it with every choice you make.

XVI

The Power of Prayer- A Quiet Force That Changes Everything

Prayer isn't about fancy words or folded hands at the perfect hour. It's not about asking for things like it's a wish list. No, my dear, it's much deeper than that. Prayer is the quiet ache in your chest when life feels too heavy. It's the soft sigh of your soul reaching out not always with words, but always with truth. Sometimes, it's just sitting still and letting your heart speak in its own way.

You see, in a world that never stops buzzing, rushing, shouting... prayer is your gentle pause. It's where you stop the world for a moment, take a breath, and remember who you are and whose you are. When everything feels upside down, prayer is what steadies you. It's not about being perfect or having all the answers. It's about coming as you are, even with messy thoughts and shaky faith.

I pray for all sorts of reasons. When I'm scared. When I'm grateful. When I just need to cry and don't want anyone else to see. Sometimes I don't even say anything I just sit with God and let Him hold me. That's enough. And when I rise, I feel a little lighter, a little braver.

Don't you think the soul needs that? A place to rest. To remember. To feel heard. Whether you call it prayer or reflection or just talking to the sky, it's all the same, your heart, finding its way home.

And don't you worry if you have doubts now and then. Even the strongest faith has its quiet questions. But choosing to pray anyway? That, my love, is trust. And that trust... it'll carry you further than you know.So hush the noise sometimes. Sit down. Breathe. And pray. Not because you *have to*, but because your soul *wants to*.

Practical Benefits of Prayer:

- **Mental Clarity**: Taking time to pray helps silence the noise. It calms the mind and gives space for clear thinking.
- **Emotional Healing**: Prayer allows people to release pain, anxiety, and anger.
- **Direction**: It's often in stillness that the next right step becomes clear.
- **Inner Strength**: Prayer doesn't always change the situation, but it often changes *you*.

Scientific Perspective

Modern research has started to catch up with ancient wisdom. Studies have shown that:

- Prayer and meditation reduce stress by lowering cortisol levels.
- It improves emotional regulation, which helps in relationships and decision-making.
- People who pray or meditate regularly tend to report higher life satisfaction and emotional resilience.

Prayer activates regions of the brain associated with compassion, empathy, and self-awareness tools that are deeply needed in today's fast-paced world.

Prayer isn't magic. It's not a vending machine where you insert a request and get what you want.It's a relationship, a practice, a discipline.Prayer isn't about controlling outcomes,it's about connecting to a greater source of wisdom and peace.Sometimes, the answer is yes. Sometimes, it's no. Sometimes, it's *not yet*. But always, it transforms us.

Real Life Stories: Purpose in Practice

"Sometimes God will put a Goliath in your life for you to find the David within you."

Alignment isn't just theoretical, it's visible in the lives of those who've surrendered and stayed the course.

Oprah Winfrey was once told she was unfit for television. But she remained prayerful, deeply aligned with her purpose, and allowed divine timing to elevate her. Her success was not just talent, it was timing and trust.

Steve Harvey lived in his car before becoming a household name. He credits his journey not just to persistence but to prayer. When nothing made sense, he chose faith over fear, and alignment did what hustle alone could not.

Nelson Mandela, despite 27 years of unjust imprisonment, found strength in soul-alignment and forgiveness. What could have broken him, built him. What was meant to confine him, prepared him to lead a nation.

Their stories remind us: the path to greatness is rarely convenient, but it is always intentional.

You Can't See Is Already Moving

You may not understand the delays. You may feel overlooked, stuck, or forgotten. But heaven is never idle. What looks like silence is often sacred preparation. What feels like rejection may actually be redirection. What you can't see is often doing the deepest work within and around you.

"When the time is right, I, the Lord, will make it happen."- **Isaiah 60:22**

Prayer won't always change your circumstances immediately, but it will always shift your posture. And when your posture is rooted in faith, peace, and surrender, you move from striving to receiving, from chasing to attracting, from surviving to soaring.

So wherever you are in your journey, pause. Reflect. Realign. *Don't chase. Align.*

Your breakthrough isn't running away, it's waiting for the version of you who is spiritually ready to walk into it.

If you're chasing peace, healing, direction, or strength, try this:

Pause. Breathe. Pray.

You don't need to be religious to pray.

You don't need to have it all together.

You just need to be willing to pause, be real, and let go.

Prayer is the most *humble* act, but it creates the most *powerful* results. It's the invisible root that produces visible fruit. And in times of uncertainty, pressure, or pain, it's not weakness to pray, it's wisdom. You might be surprised what happens when you stop trying to carry it all alone.

Faith is the fuel that keeps you moving when nothing visible is changing. It is not blind belief; it is focused trust. Faith doesn't ignore reality, it defies limitation. It is the confidence

that even when circumstances scream "impossible," faith whispers "not yet." It allows you to stand tall in storms, hold joy in waiting, and believe that the unseen is more powerful than the visible.

"Faith is taking the first step even when you don't see the whole staircase." *Martin Luther King Jr.*

Simple Ways to Practice Prayer

You don't need the perfect words. You don't need to follow a script. What matters is sincerity and consistency.Here are simple ways to incorporate prayer into your daily life:

1. Start the Day in Stillness: Even 3 minutes of quiet prayer or reflection before you check your phone can change your mental state.
2. Gratitude Prayer: End your day by naming 3 things you're thankful for. This builds joy and resets your focus.
3. Decision Time Prayer: Before making a big choice, pause. Ask for wisdom, clarity, and peace in your decision.
4. Stress Relief Prayer: In tense moments, close your eyes and take a deep breath. Whisper a short prayer for peace or guidance.
5. Walking Prayer: Reflect while walking. Let your steps be matched with slow, intentional thoughts or affirmations.

The Social Wisdom – Building Better Bonds How to navigate relationships, kindness, community, and authentic connections.

XVII

Be Kind

"Kindness is the language which the deaf can hear and the blind can see." – Mark Twain

Oh honey, kindness? That's the one language you don't need Rosetta Stone (a metaphor for anything that serves as a key to understanding a complex problem or hidden knowledge) for. Everyone understands it, from a toddler in a tantrum to a grandpa in grump mode. It's your way of saying, "Hey, I see you, and I care," without needing to shout it from the rooftops. Kindness doesn't need glitter or spotlights, just a heart that's working properly.

Science and surveys have already told us kind people are the happiest! Why? Because giving feels good. It tickles the soul! It's like feeding your heart a warm cardamom tea. Jackie Chan said it best: "Sometimes it takes only one act of kindness and caring to change a person's life." One kind word could be the nudge that stops someone from giving up. That's powerful stuff and cheaper than therapy!

Kindness doesn't need to be dramatic. Hold a door. Offer a smile. Say "thank you" like you mean it. No need to buy roses for the whole neighborhood, just don't bite someone's head off when they're already having a bad day. Wayne Dyer said, "When given the choice between being right or being kind, choose kind." And let me tell you, being right won't keep you warm at night, but being kind just might earn you a surprise cup of tea.

Let me give you a practical example. Say you're riding your bicycle and trip over a stone. Instead of cursing it, why not pause and move it so the next poor soul doesn't tumble? That, my dear, is quiet kindness, and it feels better than honking at slow walkers.

And oh, please, kindness even to those who don't deserve it? Especially them. That's the secret ingredient. And watch your words! Words aren't just air, they're bricks and people carry those bricks in their hearts for years. So before you call someone "lazy," "ugly," or "weird," ask yourself if your words are building or bulldozing.

"Be kind, for everyone you meet is fighting a hard battle." – Plato
And Grandma would say, "...and some of them are doing it without snacks or a nap, so go easy!"

Let's talk about sweet Aro. He was bullied for his looks in school. Grew up, worked on himself, healed some wounds. But then, one careless comment "You're ugly" boom! All those old scars split open. That's the thing about words, sweetheart: they're like hot oil, handle with care, or someone's getting burned.

"Kind words can be short and easy to speak, but their echoes are truly endless." – Mother Teresa And endless they are, darling. You might forget what you wore last Tuesday, but you'll remember the one kind sentence that lifted you when you were low. Kindness sticks. Meanness sticks too, but in a bad, chewed-gum-on-your-shoe kind of way.

These days, we see too much nastiness online, people throwing daggers from behind fake profiles like it's a sport. But listen to your old gran: what you throw out comes back. Maybe not today, but eventually. Kindness invites kindness. Negativity? That's like putting spoiled milk in your tea ruins everything.

A small act of kindness each day? It's better than vitamins.
And if you feel like saying something nasty, write it on paper, crumple it up, and toss it. Trust me, it's better out of your heart and into the trash.

Grandma's Sweet Little Acts of Kindness List
(Stick it on your fridge!)

- Spend time with your grandparents (especially the wise and fabulous ones). Rub their legs and collect blessings. Win-win!
  - Listen without interrupting, your ears won't fall off, promise.
  - Encourage someone who's struggling, even superheroes have off days.
  - Say "thank you" for the small things. Gratitude is like seasoning, makes life taste better.
  - Practice patience, even with that cousin who takes forever to text back.
  - Help strangers when you can, not for applause, just because it's good manners.

· Buy tea for that old man outside the bakery, he's someone's grandpa.
· Leave sweet comments online, no need to spread sourness. Life already has lemons.

Kindness Is... (according to Grandma's Recipe Book)

· Encouragement to those still trying
· Food for the hungry even if it's just the last biscuit
· Comfort for the lonely
· Hope for the hopeless
· Warmth for the forgotten
· Balm for the broken-hearted
· Respect for the downtrodden
· Love for the lost
· Happiness for anyone still breathing

Darling, if we all just did **one** act of kindness a day, the world would look like Grandma's garden in spring, blooming and buzzing with joy. We don't need to fix everyone's problems, but we sure as sugar don't need to add to them. Your words are powerful. Use them like Grandma uses turmeric with care, and only to heal.

Hurtful jokes? No thank you. Making one person laugh while another person cries? That's not comedy, that's cruelty in costume. Don't do it.

Choose kindness, sweetpea. It's free, it's healing, and it never goes out of style. Like Mother Teresa said, "Spread love everywhere you go. Let no one ever come to you without leaving happier." So go out there. Be someone's warm blanket on a cold day. Give without counting. Love without limit. And speak with the kind of softness that stays with people long after you're gone. Because when you choose kindness, you're not just being nice. You're being powerful. Sugar, kindness might not pay the bills, but it'll make the world rich in all the ways that truly matter.

The Science Behind Kindness: Why Being Nice is Actually Really Smart

Sure, Grandma always said, "Be kind, it's good for the soul." But guess what? Science says it's good for your brain, your body, and your life too. Kindness isn't just fluff and rainbows, it's hardwired into us, and it's one of the most powerful (and underrated) tools for a better, happier life.

Let's break it down:

1. Kindness Releases the "Happy Chemicals"

When you do something kind, hold a door, offer a compliment, help someone carry groceries your brain releases a delicious cocktail of feel-good chemicals:

- **Dopamine**: As discussed earlier this is your brain's "reward chemical." It makes you feel pleasure, satisfaction, and even a little euphoria. That's why kindness can feel addictive in a really good way.
- **Serotonin**: This is your "mood stabilizer." Kindness boosts serotonin levels, which improves your overall mood and emotional well-being.
- **Oxytocin**: Known as the "love hormone," oxytocin increases trust and strengthens relationships. It also reduces blood pressure and promotes heart health.

So basically, one kind act is like giving your brain a mini spa day.

2. Helper's High: The Scientific Buzz from Doing Good (Discussed earlier)

Ever helped someone and walked away feeling *weirdly amazing*? That's not coincidence, it's called the **"helper's high."**

Studies show that helping others triggers the brain's reward center, creating a burst of joy and satisfaction. One study from Emory University found that *acting generously* activates the same parts of the brain as eating chocolate or winning money.

Translation: kindness is pleasure-packed without the calories or price tag.

3. Kindness is Contagious (in a Good Way)

Psychologists call this the **"ripple effect."** When you witness or receive kindness, you're more likely to pass it on. One smile turns into ten. One thoughtful gesture creates a chain reaction. This isn't just poetic, it's been proven in countless behavioral studies.

Imagine if every small kindness you did sparked five more. The impact multiplies like magic.

4. Kindness Reduces Stress and Anxiety

When you focus on others in a caring way, your own worries often take a back seat. Studies have shown that people who engage in regular acts of kindness experience **less stress, lower cortisol levels**, and fewer symptoms of anxiety and depression.

In one study, people who did kind acts for others reported a *noticeable drop in their own daily stress* sometimes in just a week.

So next time life feels overwhelming, do something kind. It's like pressing a reset button for your soul.

5. Kindness Strengthens Your Immune System

Yep, being nice actually helps your body *fight off colds*. Oxytocin (that love hormone again!) reduces inflammation, lowers blood pressure, and boosts immunity.

Volunteering or even simple acts like writing thank-you notes have been linked to **longer lifespans** and **healthier hearts**. Being kind might not give you abs, but it could help you live longer and with more joy.

6. Kindness Improves Relationships and Social Bonds

Humans are wired for connection, and kindness is the glue that holds relationships together. Psychologists say kindness is one of the top predictors of strong, lasting friendships and romantic partnerships.

In fact, kindness is often ranked higher than attractiveness or status when it comes to what people want in a partner or friend.

Think of kindness as emotional gravity it pulls people toward you.

The Psychology of Kindness: What the Experts Say

- **Martin Seligman**, the founder of *Positive Psychology*, lists kindness as one of the 24 core character strengths that contribute most to a meaningful life.
- According to the **Broaden-and-Build Theory** by Barbara Fredrickson, positive emotions (like those sparked by kindness) broaden our awareness, enhance creativity, and build lasting mental resources like resilience and coping skills.

Kindness is not just a virtue; it's a quiet revolution. It may not make headlines or trend on social media, but its effects are long-lasting and soul-deep. It's about doing good without expecting anything in return, as Princess Diana so beautifully put it: *"Carry out a random act of kindness, with no expectation of reward, safe in the knowledge that one day someone might do the same for you."* Each time you choose compassion over criticism, empathy over ego, or gentleness over judgment, you water the seeds of love in the world.

Even a small act can warm a heavy heart. A simple compliment, a helping hand, or a patient ear, these are the true agents of change. As the Japanese proverb says, *"One kind word can warm three winter months."* We often think we need grand gestures to make a difference, but the truth is, kindness shines brightest in the small, unnoticed moments. As the Dalai Lama wisely said, *"Be kind whenever possible. It is always possible."*

When we choose to speak words that are both true and kind, we create healing, both in others and within ourselves. As Buddha said, *"When words are both true and kind, they can change the world."* So often, we underestimate the power of a kind word, a warm smile, or a listening heart. *"Too often we underestimate the power of a touch, a smile, a kind word, a listening ear, an honest compliment... all of which have the potential to turn a life around,"* wrote Leo Buscaglia. These everyday choices ripple outward, affecting lives we may never fully realize.

Because let's face it we're all carrying something. Everyone you meet is navigating their own silent battle. Kindness isn't about fixing people; it's about understanding, as Charles Glassman reminds us: *"Kindness begins with the understanding that we all struggle."*

The Bible also speaks clearly and beautifully about kindness. "Those who are kind benefit themselves, but the cruel bring ruin on themselves" (Proverbs 11:17). And, "Whoever is kind to the poor lends to the LORD, and he will reward them for what they have done" (Proverbs 19:17). These are not just poetic sayings they are promises. Even Proverbs 3:3 tells us, "Let love and faithfulness never leave you; bind them around your neck, write them on the tablet of your heart."

Listen sugarplum, life's too short to be mean and too beautiful to be bitter. Be kind. Always. You'll sleep better, laugh louder, and your wrinkles will come from smiling, not frowning. And who knows? That person you were kind to in line today might be the reason someone else doesn't give up tomorrow. So pass it on like extra butter on paratha. Let kindness be your legacy.

XVIII

Be Honest, Love

"Truthfulness is the foundation of all human virtues." – 'Abdu'l-Bahá

Now listen, baby, sit down, take a deep breath, and let your grandma tell you something most people spend their whole lives avoiding: Be honest. Not just when it's easy. Especially when it's hard. That's when it counts. That's when it makes you who you are. You know, honesty can feel like a big mountain to climb. I see that. Many of us, long before we even learned how to spell "truth," were already being taught how to lie. And no, not because we were bad, but because we were scared. Scared of punishment. Scared of being called *bad*. And sweetheart, this starts early, so early. Sometimes it's not even what our parents say, it's how they react. That look in their eyes when we admit something wrong? That's enough to teach a child, *"Uh-oh. Better keep quiet next time."*

Let Grandma tell you a little secret that nobody wants to admit out loud: most lies aren't born from wickedness, they're born from fear. Children lie because they don't want to lose love. They don't want to be seen as *bad*. When all you're ever praised for is being "good," well then, you'll do anything to protect that label. Even if it means hiding the truth. Even if it means lying.

But darling, life isn't as simple as *good or bad, success or failure.* No, no. That's not how God made us. We are complex, messy, brilliant, flawed creatures just trying our best. Sometimes we fall. Sometimes we get back up. And sometimes we lie, not because we want to but because we were taught that the truth is dangerous. But sugar, let me tell you something your grandma knows from a lifetime of watching people: the truth is not dangerous. The absence of it is.

"The truth is rarely pure and never simple." - Oscar Wilde

Oscar had it right. The truth is messy. But so is life. You're not here to be perfect, you're here to grow. You're not here to never make mistakes, you're here to learn from them.

See, every child is born like a blank notebook *tabula rasa*, as that John Locke fellow said. And everything written on you by family, by school, by culture can be rewritten. I don't care how deeply it's carved into your story. You can pick up the pen today and say, *"This is not who I choose to be anymore."* That's power, darling. That's what your grandma calls *grace*.

And bless those parents. Most of them mean well. They just pass on what they learned. But if they react to your mistakes with fear, with anger, labelling you as "bad", they plant little seeds of shame. And shame is a sticky thing. It grows wild and fast and wraps around your self-worth like ivy.

So here's what I want you to do if you're ever a parent, or a mentor, or just someone who holds space for another soul: lead with kindness, not condemnation. Catch them in a mistake? Don't destroy their spirit. Don't say, "You're bad." Say, "That was a bad choice, but I love you. Let's make it right." Teach them that one moment doesn't define their worth.

Because if they believe that being "good" is all that matters, they'll start cutting corners. Lying. Pretending. And what's the point of reaching a "right" destination if the whole journey was walked with lies? Sweetheart, the road matters as much as where it leads.

"Honesty is the best policy."- Benjamin Franklin

You've heard that before, haven't you? And you rolled your eyes a little, didn't you? But your grandma is here to tell you, Benji wasn't lying. That phrase has survived generations for a reason. It's not just about being moral, it's practical. You don't have to remember your lies if you're telling the truth. You don't have to hide who you are when your actions match your words. That, my love, is freedom.

Honesty and Self Respect

Now listen close, sugar, this one's tender but tough. You cannot, and I mean cannot, respect yourself if you're lying to yourself. You might fool the world with a smile, you might even convince others you're fine, but deep down, your soul always knows. That little ache in your chest? That nagging feeling that something's off? That's your integrity tapping you on the shoulder, whispering, *"What's up filthy?"*

See, when your words don't match your actions, when you say you value peace, but keep chasing chaos, when you promise growth, but cling to comfort, your spirit notices. And it hurts. Because self-respect isn't built on achievement or applause. It's built on alignment. When who you are, what you believe, and how you show up all stand in the same light.

"Truthfulness is the cornerstone in character, and if it be not firmly laid in youth, there will ever after be a weak spot in the foundation."- Jefferson Davis

And honey, that weak spot? It doesn't stay small. It grows. It cracks your confidence. It leaks into your relationships. It chips away at the joy you're meant to live with. But here's the good news: so does strength. When you choose truth, even the hard kind you start building something solid and something that lasts.

Being true to yourself means saying no when your soul says no. It means leaving spaces that don't see your worth. It means calling yourself out not to shame, but to grow. It's waking up in the morning and looking in the mirror with a quiet kind of pride. Not because you've got it all together, but because you're not pretending. And let me tell you, that kind of peace? It's rare. It's rich. It's worth every uncomfortable truth you had to face to get there.

When you live in truth, you sleep deeper. You breathe easier. You carry yourself taller. You stop chasing validation because you've already made peace with the most important person in the room you. And that shows. People can feel it. They trust you, not because you're flawless, but because you're real. And in a world full of polished masks, a real one? A true one? Baby, that's gold.

So choose honesty, not just with others, but with yourself. Especially with yourself. That's where the real transformation begins. That's where respect is born. And that's where your best life starts to take shape not from being perfect, but from being true.

Honesty with Kindness

Now listen here, sugar, don't you go using honesty like it's a hammer, swinging it around and smashing people just because you think you're "just being real." That's not honesty that's just plain hurtfulness dressed up in self righteous clothes. True honesty? It doesn't stomp in with boots on and leave people bleeding. It walks in gently, with soft hands and a warm heart. It knows when to speak and when to hush.

Being truthful isn't about blurting out everything that pops into your head. It's about timing, tone, and tenderness. It's about knowing that people are delicate sometimes, and words, well, they can either heal or harm. You have to choose carefully.

So before you go saying your piece, run your words through grandma's three wise gates, would you? Ask yourself:

Is it true? Is it necessary? Is it kind?– Rumi

And I mean all three, not just one. If it's true but it's gonna cut someone up like broken glass, you hold it in and find a softer way. If it's not necessary, don't stir the pot. If it ain't kind, then honey, don't say it at all.

Because honesty without kindness? That's just cruelty pretending to be noble. But when you mix truth with tenderness, now that's real magic. That's how you build trust instead of burning bridges. Speak truth, yes, but speak it like you love the person listening. That's the kind of honesty that leaves people better, not broken.

The Role of Honesty in a Complex World

Now sit down for a second, baby, and really take a look around. The world's gotten noisy, hasn't it? Everyone's busy curating their lives, filters, highlights without the lows, smiles masking struggles. You scroll and see perfection, but behind it? So often, it's just fear dressed up pretty. People showing you who they *want* to be, not who they *are*. And in this sea of polished pretense, do you know what's rare? Someone who's *real*. Someone who dares to be honest, especially when it's inconvenient, unpopular, or downright terrifying.

"Honesty and transparency make you vulnerable. Be honest and transparent anyway." - Mother Teresa

That kind of honesty? It takes guts. It's not loud, but it's powerful. It means telling the truth even when it shakes your voice. It means standing by your values when no one's clapping. It's not about being brutally blunt or always "speaking your mind", it's about being true to your spirit. It's about looking in the mirror at night and smiling, not because you got everything right, but because you stayed in alignment with your heart.

But hear me out, sweetheart truth is only part of the story. *Kindness* is the other. You don't need to throw truth like a grenade to prove your strength. Sometimes the real power lies in choosing the right moment, the gentle tone, the gracious silence. Pick kindness. Always pick kindness. Not instead of honesty, but alongside it. That's the secret sauce. That's what makes truth healing, not harming.

"To believe in something, and not to live it, is dishonest." – Mahatma Gandhi

So don't just wear your values like a badge, *live* them. Let your actions speak your truth louder than any speech. Be the kind of soul your future children can look up to, your younger self would be proud of, and your heart can rest easy with. Not perfect. Not always polished. But honest. Gentle. Whole.

Because at the end of the day, sugar, when the lights go out and the noise dies down, you're left alone with *you*. Not the mask you wore. Not the role you played. Just *you*. And that version of you quiet, real, imperfect, beautiful you owe that soul the truth.

Let's talk science for a moment:

According to Carl Jung, living an inauthentic life, one where we reject our truth to please others or avoid discomfort leads to a disconnect between our conscious identity and what he calls the "shadow self." That shadow holds all the truth we refuse to acknowledge. And the more we repress it, the more it leaks out through anxiety, anger, self-doubt, or shame.

But when you live honestly? You integrate those shadows. You stop pretending. And that's when peace begins.

Psychologist Leon Festinger introduced the concept of Cognitive Dissonance, the inner tension you feel when your actions don't match your beliefs. For example, if you say you value honesty but lie to avoid confrontation, your brain doesn't let you off the hook. It creates discomfort. That's your integrity knocking, baby. And you can't find peace until you open the door.

Maslow's Hierarchy of Needs puts *self-actualization* becoming your truest, highest self right at the top. But you can't get there through pretending. Honesty is the ladder. If you're lying to stay safe or fit in, you're stuck on the lower rungs, chasing approval instead of purpose.

And let's not forget Erik Erikson's theory of psychosocial development. He believed that every stage of life comes with a psychological task. In adulthood, the challenge is to live with integrity versus despair. That means being able to look back on your life and say, "I was true. I lived honestly." Not perfectly, but with honesty and intention.

Now, how does all this tie into success and peace?

Authentic Leadership Theory teaches that the most effective, trustworthy leaders are not the ones who hide behind masks, but the ones who show up with transparency, consistency, and values. When you're honest, people trust you. When you're consistent, people believe you. And when you're real, people follow you.

Now don't make me come back and repeat myself, darling. Life ain't a costume party you don't need to dress up your soul to impress anyone. Be honest. Not just 'cause it's noble, but because it saves you a hell of a lot of drama. Lies are like cheap perfume, they don't last, and they stink up everything on the way out. You wanna sleep like a then tell the truth. Live the truth. Even when it's messy. Even when it isn't cute. But don't forget, wrap that truth in kindness, like a good pie in a warm crust. 'Cause honesty without kindness? That's just rudeness with good PR. So straighten that back, speak your truth with heart, and let the world adjust. Grandma's proud of you already.

Morality Is a Privilege: Practice Honesty with Compassion

While honesty is vital, it's important to recognize that morality, like many virtues is often a privilege. Not everyone has the same capacity to act with integrity when survival is on the line. For some, lying isn't a choice, it's a means to protect themselves in an unsafe environment. A child might lie to avoid punishment. A worker might hide the truth to keep their job. A friend might avoid honesty out of fear of abandonment. These are not failures of character; they are reflections of the circumstances that shaped them. Grandma would say, "Don't judge the flower before you've felt the storm that bent its stem." Being honest doesn't mean we get to become self-righteous. It means we must also be understanding. Real honesty carries humility, an awareness that not everyone has had the safety or support to live by the truth. As we grow in integrity, let us also grow in empathy. Instead of shaming others into truth, create the kind of safe spaces where honesty can finally feel like home.

Gentle Daily Habits to Strengthen Your Honesty (Grandma-Approved!)

1. **Start with Yourself:**
   Before you can be honest with others, be honest with yourself. Each morning, take a quiet moment to ask: *How am I really feeling today?* Grandma always said, "You can't fix what you pretend isn't broken."

2. **Keep One Small Promise Daily:**
   Whether it's drinking more water or calling your friend back, keep one small promise to yourself each day. It builds self-trust. "If you say you'll eat the apple, don't go sneaking for the laddu," Grandma would wink.

3. **Pause Before You Speak:**
   Before blurting out anything, ask yourself: *Is it true? Is it necessary? Is it kind?* This filter isn't just wise, it's kind hearted honesty in action.

4. **Write It Out:**
   A quick nightly journal helps you reflect on your day: Were you honest?

Where did you struggle? Writing it down helps you catch patterns. Paper listens better than your partner.

5. **Catch the Little White Lies:**

   They sneak in easily, "I'm on my way" when you're not. Start small: when you're tempted to lie, try silence or truth delivered gently. Progress over perfection.

6. **Own Your Mistakes Quickly:**

   If you mess up, admit it early and with grace. No one likes a cover-up. Confession is good for the soul, and saves a lot of explaining.

7. **Surround Yourself with Truth-Tellers:**

   Spend time with people who value honesty and growth. It rubs off. Choose friends who lovingly tell you the truth not those who lie or sabotage.

8. **Practice Saying "I Don't Know" or "I Was Wrong":**

   These phrases are not weaknesses, they are signs of strength. Grandma Sniffa would say, "Only fools pretend to know everything. Smart folks ask, learn, and grow."

9. **Pray or Meditate for Clarity:**

   Ask for strength to stay honest in tough moments. When your spirit is clear, your truth flows easier. As Grandma would whisper before bed, "Speak to God about the truth, and He'll help you live it."

XIX

The Art of Coexisting

"You must not lose faith in humanity. Humanity is an ocean; if a few drops of the ocean are dirty, the ocean does not become dirty." – Mahatma Gandhi

People often mistake coexistence for people pleasing, but they couldn't be more different. People pleasing is like wearing a mask, constantly changing to fit what others want until you lose sight of who you really are. It's born from a hunger for approval, often leaving your own needs and peace behind. Coexistence, however, is a quiet power. It's the art of standing tall in your own truth while offering kindness and respect to others. As Stephen Covey wisely said, *"You can't be successful with other people if you haven't paid the price of it with yourself."* Grandma would chuckle and say, "Child, don't water yourself down to make someone else's garden grow. True strength is in knowing your worth and sharing your light without burning yourself out." When you embrace coexistence, you don't just survive relationships you thrive in them, grounded in authenticity, compassion, and firm boundaries that protect your heart.

The Fluid Nature of People

People are beautifully complex and constantly evolving. To judge someone solely based on one action or interaction is to overlook the vast spectrum of their character. The person who may have wronged you could simultaneously be a source of joy, love, and inspiration to someone else. As Oscar Wilde insightfully observed, "Every saint has a past, and every sinner has a future."

This understanding encourages empathy and a broader perspective on human nature. Each of us is a different version of ourselves in different contexts and relationships, shaped by our experiences, choices, and environments. No one remains static; we are all works in progress, continuously growing and learning. As Maya Angelou said, "I did then what I knew how to do. Now that I know better, I do better." Recognizing this ever changing nature of humanity fosters kindness and patience, reminding us that we, too, are more than our mistakes and have the capacity to transform. We must always remember that every person carries a story far deeper than what we see on the surface.

Responding to Judgment: Family, Culture, and Perspective

A common struggle is dealing with judgment or unsolicited advice from loved ones, especially in cultures with strong family ties. For instance, parents or grandparents might express views rooted in their generation's beliefs, which may conflict with modern values.

During a conversation with my best friend Chu, I was venting about how my family insisted I get married simply because society deemed it necessary. I felt frustrated and misunderstood. Chu, with her characteristic wit, asked me, "Would you be okay if your child identified as a cockroach?" I immediately said no. Then she asked me to sit with that thought. That moment was eye opening. I realized that just as I struggle to accept something so radically different from my beliefs, my parents struggle with accepting my choices because they challenge their belief system. It's not about one being right or wrong, it's about how deeply ingrained perspectives can be. To my parents, getting married late isn't "normal" because of the societal norms they grew up with, just as identifying as a cockroach might challenge what I consider "normal." This realization taught me that everyone operates within the framework of their understanding, shaped by their experiences, culture, and values. By empathizing with their viewpoint, even when it conflicts with my own, I found a sense of peace. Understanding doesn't mean agreeing; it means acknowledging that their beliefs, like mine, stem from deeply rooted perspectives. Recognizing this can help us respond with patience rather than anger.

Child, remember this: just like you wouldn't throw out the whole basket because of a few bruised apples, don't toss out people or relationships just because of a few misunderstandings. Patience and a gentle heart go a long way.

So when the world pushes and pulls, remind yourself: coexistence is not about losing yourself to please others; it's about standing firm in who you are, while making room for others to be who they are. It's the art of harmony without sacrifice. And if you ever feel lost in the noise, take a deep breath and listen, sometimes the quiet between words carries the deepest understanding. Because, as Grandma always says with a wink, "A little kindness, sprinkled with wisdom and a dash of patience, can turn any storm into a gentle rain."

Understanding Coexistence Through Derrida's Concept of Deconstruction

To truly grasp the concept of coexistence, we can draw inspiration from Jacques Derrida's philosophy of deconstruction. Imagine drawing a circle on a piece of paper and marking a center point. Now, ask yourself: why did you choose that particular spot as the center? Perhaps it's because society or prior learning taught you to see it that way. But what if we unlearned that conditioning? If five people were asked to mark their own centers, each would likely choose a different spot, shaped by their unique perspectives.

This simple exercise is just like life:

- Each person perceives the world through their own lens, molded by upbringing, culture, and personal experiences.
- No single "center" or truth is absolute or universal.

Derrida's profound statement, *"The center is not the center,"* encapsulates this idea beautifully. It suggests that what we often consider fixed or central is merely one interpretation among many. Life is a blend of perspectives and interpretations, none of which hold ultimate authority.

Similarly, coexistence demands that we acknowledge and honor the fact that others have their own "centers" their opinions, choices, beliefs, and truths all shaped by their distinct experiences. Expecting everyone to align with your perspective is not only unrealistic but also a subtle form of control. As philosopher Marcus Aurelius observed, *"Everything we hear is an opinion, not a fact. Everything we see is a perspective, not the truth."*

True coexistence lies in embracing this diversity of thought and perspective. It means respecting the individuality and autonomy of others while staying true to your own values. As Mahatma Gandhi wisely put it, *"Honest disagreement is often a good sign of progress."* Progress is not achieved through conformity but through understanding, acceptance, and the willingness to learn from each other's differences.

Grandma would lean in with a twinkle in her eye and say,
"Child, think of this world like a big patchwork quilt, every piece is different,

stitched with its own color and story. You don't have to make every patch the same, but you do have to learn to hold them all together with love and patience. That's the true heart of coexistence."

So, remember: the beauty of life is found not in everyone sharing the same center, but in the dance of many centers, moving together in respect and harmony. And if ever you're confused or frustrated by differences, take a deep breath and listen, because often, the quiet between our words is where understanding quietly grows.

Letting Go of the Illusion of Control

One of the greatest barriers to coexistence is the desire to control others. While it may sometimes feel like an act of love or empowerment, trying to dictate someone else's thoughts, actions, or choices is ultimately both selfish and futile. As Epictetus, the Stoic philosopher, wisely remarked, *"We cannot choose our external circumstances, but we can always choose how we respond to them."* True coexistence begins the moment we release the need to control others and instead turn our attention to how we respond and act ourselves.

When we let go of this need for control, we free ourselves from unnecessary frustration and pain. Evelyn Beatrice Hall, in her famous words attributed to Voltaire, beautifully expressed this idea: *"I disapprove of what you say, but I will defend to the death your right to say it."* Disagreement need not be bitter or hostile; it can be spoken with respect and dignity.

Carl Jung reminds us, *"Everything that irritates us about others can lead us to an understanding of ourselves."* When we recognize that others have the right to their perspectives even when they clash wildly with ours, we open the door to empathy, patience, and deeper self awareness. Coexisting is not about forcing our beliefs on others but embracing the beautiful diversity of thought, knowing that true strength is found in unity without uniformity.

I would say,

"Child, trying to control others is like holding water in your fist, the tighter you squeeze, the more slips away. Let go a little, and you'll find your hands are free to hold what truly matters. Love isn't about making others fit your mold; it's about letting them be themselves, while you be your best self. That's the true magic of coexistence."

So, remember: the power to live peacefully with others starts with the courage to release control, the grace to accept differences, and the wisdom to protect your own peace. In this way, coexistence becomes not just possible, but a beautiful dance where every step respects the rhythm of many hearts.

Practical Steps for Mindful Coexistence

Practice Empathy:

When someone expresses a hurtful opinion, pause and step into their shoes. Consider their experiences, upbringing, and the influences that shaped their beliefs. Empathy is the bridge to understanding. As Harper Lee beautifully wrote in *To Kill a Mockingbird*:*"You never really understand a person until you consider things from his point of view, until you climb into his skin and walk around in it."*

Let Go of Expectations:

Expecting others to think, feel, or act as you do often leads to disappointment. Instead, embrace the uniqueness of each individual. As Donald Miller wisely put it, *"When you stop expecting people to be perfect, you can like them for who they are."* By releasing rigid expectations, you open yourself up to appreciating people as they are, not as you wish them to be. After all, as the saying goes, *"Expect nothing, and you'll always be pleasantly surprised."*

Respond, Don't React:

Reactions are often impulsive and fueled by emotion, while responses are thoughtful and intentional. Practice mindfulness to pause and reflect before engaging. Viktor Frankl powerfully captures this wisdom:*"Between stimulus and response, there is a space. In that space is our power to choose our response. In our response lies our growth and freedom."*

Set Boundaries:

Coexisting doesn't mean tolerating disrespect. Establish clear boundaries to protect your emotional and mental well-being while honoring the autonomy of others.As Lalah Delia aptly puts it, *"Boundaries are not a wall, they are a bridge to a better you."* Boundaries help create a space where respect and understanding can flourish, allowing both you and others to thrive without compromising your well-being.

Focus on What You Can Control:

Accept that you cannot change others or dictate their choices. Instead, redirect your energy toward how you respond and engage with them. As the famous prayer goes:*"God, grant me the serenity to accept the things I cannot change, courage to change the things I can, and wisdom to know the difference."*

Child, life's a bit like a potluck dinner. Everyone brings their own dish to the table, some sweet, some spicy, some plain strange. You don't have to eat it all, but you do need to respect what they brought. Coexisting doesn't mean you change your flavor to match everyone else. It means you show up with your best recipe, serve it with love, and leave space at the table for others to do the same. Coexisting doesn't mean compromising your values or tolerating disrespect. It's about respecting the diversity of human thought and experience while preserving your core self. It's about loving people without losing yourself in the process.As you practice coexistence, you'll find greater peace, deeper connections, and a profound appreciation for humanity's complexity. In the words of Periyar:*"Do not let anyone do your thinking for you, but also do not impose your thinking on others."*

XX

Never Underestimate the Power of Having Good People Around You

Even the Brightest Star Can't Shine in a Black Hole

"*Baby, you could be the ripest peach on the tree, and there'll still be somebody allergic to fruit.*" -Dolly Parton (and your sassy grandma)

Let me tell you something that'll save you years of heartache: No amount of hustling, praying, or people pleasing will make a toxic environment healthy. I don't care if you're the human equivalent of a solar flare, dump you in a swamp, and all you'll do is attract mosquitoes.

Listen Up, Buttercup: Your Environment is Sculpting You

That Pygmalion Effect ain't just some stuffy psychology term it's the reason why my bridge partner Mabel's grandson went from flipping burgers to running that fancy tech startup. Remember George Bernard Shaw's play Pygmalion (where that delightful *My Fair Lady* came from- beautiful song go listen)? The whole point was that Professor Higgins transformed Eliza Doolittle from a Cockney flower girl into a proper lady simply by treating her like one. As Shaw himself wrote: "The difference between a lady and a flower girl is not how she behaves, but how she's treated."

Now here's where it gets juicy, sugar - in 1968, psychologists Rosenthal and Jacobson proved this works in real life. They told teachers certain students were "intellectual bloomers" (even though they were just regular kids), and guess what? Those students' IQ scores shot up 12-15 points by year's end! Why? Because when people expect more from you, you rise to meet it. But here's the flip side - it works in reverse too. That "friend" who always says "Oh honey, be realistic" about your dreams? The aunt who clucks "We just want you to have a stable job" when you mention your business idea? They're not just being negative Nancies, they're literally programming you to stay small. Like Joel Osteen says: "You cannot hang out with negative people and expect to live a positive life."

And don't you dare think you're immune, sweet pea. Neuroscience shows that chronic exposure to naysayers:

- Floods your brain with cortisol (the stress hormone)

- Shrinks your hippocampus (that's the memory center, precious)

- Makes you 37% more likely to self sabotage (University of Michigan study)

Remember darling - you're either growing or decaying. There's no in-between. As my third husband used to say before I divorced him: *"If you're the smartest person in the room, you're in the wrong damn room."* Now go find yourself some people who look at you like you're the second coming of Jesus with a business degree.

The Strawberry Theory

Oh honey, let me tell you about strawberries and sourpusses - they've got more in common than you'd think! When I was a kid, strawberries were like edible rubies, so precious we'd eat them one nibble at a time to make 'em last. Now? I walk right past 'em at the grocery store. Why? Because all it takes is one mushy berry at the bottom of the container and - poof! - by morning your whole batch is fit for the compost heap.

And sugar, let me tell you, people work exactly the same dang way. That coworker who complains louder than my arthritic knees in winter? That cousin who could find the cloud in every silver lining? They're human rotten strawberries, and they'll spoil your whole bunch faster.

Like my dear friend Albert Einstein used to say (God rest his brilliant soul): *"Stay away from negative people. They have a problem for every solution."* And that man split the atom - he knew a thing or two about powerful forces!

Here's the bitter truth, sweet pea:

· Negativity spreads 10x faster than positivity (Harvard study says so)
· Just 15 minutes around a complainer floods your brain with stress hormones

- It takes 5 positive interactions to cancel out 1 negative one - that's why I feel wiped after brunch with Munima

Now I'm not saying you need to be Pollyanna(a character known for her consummate optimism and her ability to find something positive in every situation,). But chronic negativity? That's like emotional black mold, baby. Before you know it, you're:
· Rolling your eyes at good news
· Calling optimism "naive"
· Forgetting how to smile without sarcasm

Remember darling - life's too short for bad fruit and bitter people. The secret to sweet strawberries (and sweeter relationships)? Don't let the rotten ones linger. Toss 'em fast and savor the good ones!

Emotional Contagion: Not Catching Other People's Funk

Well butter call me a scientist - turns out emotions spread faster than my gossip at bridge club! This "Emotional Contagion" business ain't just some fancy psychology term - it's why you leave some people feeling like you just won the lottery and others like you need a shower and a stiff drink. Here's the tea, sweet pea: your brain's got these little things called mirror neurons that make you unconsciously copy the moods around you like Munima tries to copy me, trust me she even got herself a 35 year old stud, not as hot but still Munima is copy cat. Studies show:

- It takes just $1/20^{th}$ of a second to "catch" someone's emotions
- Negative emotions spread 3x faster than positive ones
- Chronic complainers literally rewire your brain for pessimism (University of Indiana proved it!)

As my girl Oprah says: *"Surround yourself with only people who are going to lift you higher."* And that woman built an empire while making couch chats feel like church - she knows what's what!

The Honeybees: People who leave you buzzing with energy (keep 'em close)
The Lemons: Folks who leave a sour taste (perfect for water, not for your soul)
The Vinegar: Toxic types who pickle your spirit (toss 'em out like expired milk)

Remember what happened when I let Sad Sally join book club? Within a month we'd switched from reading romance to complaining about our knee pains! That's emotional contagion, sugar - as real as my arthritis when it rains. Your vibe attracts your tribe, and your tribe determines your vibe. So ask yourself: *"Do I feel like the best version of myself around these people?"* If not, well the door's that way, darling.

Now go find your sparkle people, the ones who make your mirror neurons light up like my Christmas tree in December. *"You wouldn't let someone sneeze in your face without moving. Why let them spray their negativity all over your dreams?"* - Your Future Self (living her best life)

P.S. Even the Bible got it right: *"Bad company corrupts good character."* (1 Corinthians 15:33) And honey, if it's in the Good Book and science confirms it? That's what we call a mic drop.

Who Are You Letting Into Your Mental Space?

Let's be honest: some people aren't just draining, they're destructive. They're the ones who roll their eyes at your excitement, call your dreams unrealistic, and talk behind your back under the disguise of "concern." These are **emotional vampires**, people who, knowingly or not, drain your joy, crush your spirit, and leave you feeling like you're "too much" just for being you.

"Let go of the people who dull your shine, poison your spirit, and bring you drama. Cancel your subscription to their issues." – Steve Maraboli

You don't need that. You need people who *see you, hear you, and cheer for you.*

Why the Right People Matter

You ever leave a conversation feeling ten feet taller? Like suddenly, the sun's a little brighter, and your dreams don't feel so crazy anymore? That, sweetheart, isn't coincidence. That's called alignment. That's the power of being seen by the *right* people, those rare souls who pour courage into your cup without even trying. Psychologists call it Positive Peer Influence, but grandma just calls it *good company*. When you're around folks who *believe* in you, your nervous system calms down. Your self-belief stretches. You stop bracing for rejection and start preparing for greatness.

There's actual science behind it too, mirror neurons in our brains cause us to reflect the emotions and energy of the people we're around. So if you're in the company of driven, kind, soul fueling humans? You start becoming one, too. Not out of pressure but because it feels *safe* to bloom.

The right people challenge your excuses but never your worth. They won't coddle your comfort zone, but they'll never laugh at your dreams. They'll call you out when you're shrinking, remind you of who you are when you forget, and walk with you even when you're limping emotionally.

Seek out those people who make you feel more like yourself, not less. Who light a fire under your potential and help you hold your own mirror steady. And just as important? Be that person for others. Be the one who uplifts the room, who makes honesty gentle, who celebrates loudly, and listens softly.

Because at the end of the day, baby, we all rise or fall with the company we keep. And you deserve a circle that feels like sunlight.

How to Protect Your Circle

Here are a few principles to live by:

- **Audit your energy:** After spending time with someone, ask yourself: *Do I feel lighter or heavier?* That's your answer.
- **Don't confuse history with alignment:** Just because they've been in your life for 10 years doesn't mean they deserve to stay 10 more.
- **Protect your peace at all costs:** Say no to draining conversations, constant drama, and people who only call when they need something.
- **Choose alignment over attachment:** Be brave enough to outgrow people without feeling guilty.
- Make clear choices of the events and conversations you want to be a part.

Your Survival Toolkit

1. The "Plant Test"

"Would a rose bloom here?" If your workplace/relationship/friend group would kill a cactus, it's killing you too.

2. The 24-Hour Energy Audit

Track who:

Gives you energy (keep)

Drains you (limit)

Destroys you (block)

3. The "Five-Year Screw It" Rule

"Will this environment matter in five years? If not, why am I wasting five minutes?"

When to Walk Away

- When you're the only one watering the relationship
- When you have to shrink to fit in (Honey, trees don't grow taller by staying in tiny pots. Sometimes the bravest thing you can do is admit you've outgrown your environment.)
- When your gut says "run" but your guilt says "maybe" (*Pro tip: Your gut has better judgment*)

Baby, the people around you are like soil to a plant. You could be the healthiest seed, but if you're planted in toxic ground, **you will never bloom**. But if you're in fertile, nourishing soil surrounded by other growing things you'll rise, effortlessly, beautifully. So choose wisely. Your peace, your purpose, and your power depend on it.

"Show me your friends, and I'll show you your future." – Dan Pena

XXI

People Skills -The Real Secret to Success

"You can have everything in life you want, if you will just help other people get what they want."- Zig Ziglar

Baby there's something magnetic about people who know how to deal with other people. They walk into a room, and without even trying, they shift the energy. They don't demand attention they command it by simply being present, sincere, and kind.

I've never claimed to be the smartest in the room. But what I do know is this: no one makes eye contact with me and walks away without seeing every one of my teeth. That's my signature, my smile. Sounds funny, I know. But that smile? It has opened doors my degrees never could. It has started conversations that turned into collaborations. It has disarmed anger, soothed pain, and built bridges.

People often talk about IQ. But there's something far more valuable in today's world- EQ, or emotional intelligence. At its heart, EQ is the ability to understand and manage your own emotions while also being sensitive to the emotions of others. It's the foundation of all great leadership, communication, and connection.

Daniel Goleman, a leading psychologist and author of Emotional Intelligence, found that EQ accounts for 80-90% of the competencies that differentiate top performers from average. Let that sink in. It's not how much you know. It's how well you connect, respond,empathize, and engage.

Smiling: The Weapon of the Wise

"Peace begins with a smile."- Mother Teresa

Let's talk science for a second. When you smile, your brain releases dopamine and serotonin, the very same chemicals that are released when you fall in love or achieve something great. And when you make someone else smile, their brain does the same.

That means your smile isn't just a facial movement, it's emotional medicine. It's a light switch that turns on joy in dark places.

Smiling changes the way people see you. But more importantly, it changes the way you see people. I used to think some people were just mean, cold, or closed off. But the truth is, they're just waiting for someone to break the ice. Every person's 'pookie' is almost always one smile away.

What People Will Never Forget

Think about the people who have left a mark on your life. What do you remember about them?

Their resume? Their qualifications? Their income?Probably not.

You remember how they made you feel. Maybe they made you feel important. Or safe. Or accepted. Or inspired. That's the magic of people skills. It's not about you. It's about how you make others feel about themselves.

"People may hear your words, but they feel your attitude."-John C. Maxwell

I've had people come up to me years later and say, "I'll never forget the way you welcomed me," or "You made me feel seen when I really needed it." And you know what? That's my greatest achievement.

"You never really understand a person until you consider things from his point of view."
-Harper Lee

What you give doesn't have to be grand. Sometimes, what people need is not money or things, it's a warm word, a hug, a safe space, a smile that says, "You matter."

Psychological and Communication Theories That Prove People Skills Matter

1. The Halo Effect- Edward Thorndike

What it means:

The *Halo Effect* is a cognitive bias where we assume that if someone is good at one thing (like being warm or friendly), we believe they are good at everything else too (like competent, trustworthy, or smart). This means that a genuine smile, a warm tone, or a kind gesture can instantly make someone appear more capable in every area.

Application:

When you smile, listen, and treat someone with kindness, their brain automatically tags you as a good person in general. First impressions matter. Be warm, be present that first moment can shape everything that follows.

2. The Liking Principle (from Robert Cialdini's Six Principles of Persuasion)

What it means:

People are more likely to say yes to those they like. And what makes someone likable? Shared values, compliments, empathy, warmth, and the ability to make others feel important.

Application:

People buy from, support, follow, and trust those they like. If you're in sales, leadership, coaching, or even just trying to make new friends, your likability is your leverage. Be someone others enjoy being around.

"People don't care how much you know until they know how much you care." - Theodore Roosevelt

3. Maslow's Hierarchy of Needs- Abraham Maslow

What it means:

Maslow proposed that every human has a hierarchy of needs, ranging from basic survival to self-actualization. Just above food and shelter is the need for love, belonging, and connection.

Application:

If you want to reach someone's heart or even motivate them you need to meet their emotional needs first. Making someone feel like they belong or are valued instantly creates trust and loyalty.

4. Emotional Contagion Theory

What it means:

Emotions are contagious. We subconsciously mimic the facial expressions, tone, and energy of those around us. This is why one person's mood can lift or sink an entire room.

Application:

When you bring joy, laughter, and presence, others subconsciously mirror you. If you're positive, they become positive. If you're calm, they feel safe. You set the emotional tone.

5. Mirror Neurons & Empathy

Science backed concept

Mirror neurons in our brain fire not only when we perform an action, but when we see someone else doing it. These neurons are responsible for empathy, and they allow us to feel what others are feeling.

Application:

Your ability to express empathy through facial expressions, tone, and body language makes people feel understood. And when people feel understood, they trust you. This is the foundation of every lasting relationship.

6. The Law of Reciprocity

What it means:

People feel obligated to return favors, kindness, and generosity. When you give (whether it's a compliment, a smile, or time), others feel moved to give back even subconsciously.

Application:

This law works everywhere, business, networking, friendships, even in crisis. When you go first in giving love, understanding, or value, people remember it, and they return it often tenfold.

7. Self-Perception Theory - Daryl Bem

What it means:

We form attitudes based on our behavior. If we act like we are confident, happy, and connected, we begin to believe we are. Behavior shapes identity.

Application:

If you start smiling more, reaching out, giving compliments, and listening deeply, you'll start seeing yourself as a warm, charismatic person. And soon, others will too.

8. The Need to Belong Theory- Roy Baumeister & Mark Leary

What it means:

Humans have a fundamental need to feel connected. This isn't optional, it's as essential as eating or sleeping. People will go to great lengths to avoid rejection or isolation.

Application:

If you make people feel seen, heard, and included, you are giving them oxygen. And when you consistently do that, people naturally gravitate toward you.

The ability to make people feel special, understood, and valued is what opens doors, wins hearts, creates opportunities, and builds a legacy. Whether you want to lead a company, change lives, sell a product, or raise a child people skills are the secret to doing it well. I've been blessed to wear many hats, professor, student leader, DJ, coach, speaker. And through all these roles, the one thing that never failed me was my people skill. I walk into any room with the mindset that everyone is good, and even if they're not showing it right now, it's just buried beneath pain, fear, or experience.

When you approach people without judgment, they surprise you with their goodness. Believe in the good in people and they will rise to meet that belief.

That's why I say: the best skill you can develop is people skill. In sales? People skills. In marketing? People skills. In coaching? People skills. In leadership? People skills.

Every single career, relationship, and opportunity is ultimately a people game. Master this, and you win.

The Soul Level Power of Making Someone Feel Good

"The most basic of all human needs is the need to understand and be understood. The best way to understand people is to listen to them."-Ralph Nichols

It doesn't cost a thing to care. To remember names. To say thank you. To listen without interrupting. To make people feel heard. When you treat people like they matter, they come alive. And that energy always comes back to you.

You want to stand out in a crowd?

- Make others feel seen.
- Make others feel safe.
- Make others feel special.

Because *everyone* is secretly longing for that. Everyone wants to feel important. And when you give people that gift, you become unforgettable.

Practical Tools to Boost Your People Skills Today

1. Smile, even when it's hard.
   Your smile is someone else's courage.
2. Be present.
   Put away your phone. Look them in the eyes.
3. Use their name.
   It's the most beautiful word in any language.
4. Listen to understand, not to respond.
   People don't want solutions first. They want connection.
5. Show empathy.
   Even if you haven't walked in their shoes, be willing to feel what they feel.
6. Give without expectations.
   Give warmth, comfort, encouragement, it multiplies when it's

unconditional.
7. Celebrate people.
    Remember birthdays, acknowledge efforts, compliment honestly.
8. Apologize quickly.
    Owning your mistakes makes you real, not weak.

Loving people isn't always easy. Sometimes it's messy, inconvenient, or even painful. But it is always worth it. When you start viewing every person as a walking miracle, with hidden battles and unspoken dreams you'll never treat anyone the same again.

Let your smile be the spark. Let your words be the warmth. Let your presence be the peace.People skills are not just tools, they are superpowers. They make you magnetic. They make you unstoppable. And most of all, they make you human.So go on love, talk to strangers. Laugh loud. Compliment wildly. Hug freely. Love deeply. Be that one person who lights up every room, not because of your brilliance but because of your heart.

XXII

Giving: Grandma's Magic to Multiplying

"No one has ever become poor by giving." - Anne Frank

Now listen carefully, sugarplum, don't ever believe that giving makes you poor. That's like saying eating seeds will make plants grow within you. When you give, your hands don't get empty; they overflow! Like when you sneak an extra cookie to your neighbor, suddenly your own tea tastes twice as good. The people who truly understand the value of things are those who have very little. Twenty rupees might be pocket change to you, but to a hungry person, it's the difference between a full stomach and a growling hunger.

I tell you, a country that lets even one person starve has already lost the game. What kind of celebration is it when the whole nation cheers for Chandrayaan-3 landing on the moon, but a mother is begging for her child's bread here on Earth? Makes me wonder what we're really celebrating. Rockets in space, while people here shiver without blankets? If that's progress, I want my money back. If someone asks for something, give what you can, don't be counting coins like a miser guarding treasure. Be the reason someone's heart smiles today. I'm not here to talk politics or fancy speeches, just plain old kindness the kind even your grumpiest neighbor can't argue with.

Giving is like planting a magic seed; it grows into a tree that keeps giving fruit forever. You give a little, it comes back tenfold, maybe in ways you can't even imagine like when you lend sugar to a neighbor and next week they bring you extra sweets. And no, it's not always about money or things. A smile, a kind word, a little "Well done!" can turn someone's whole day around faster than tea kicks in on a Monday morning. When you see that light in their eyes, your heart feels like it's dancing. Energy is real, good energy given freely comes right back to you like a boomerang with a turbo boost.

The best kind of giving? Giving to those who can't pay you back. Anyone can give to the rich, but true generosity is feeding the hungry when they have nothing to offer you in return. Imagine this, you see a unhealthy little child, ribs showing, shivering in the cold. You run to buy some food and give it to him. His smile? Priceless. You can't buy that anywhere, no matter how many rupees you throw around and trust me, I've tried. I remember my university days in the 1970's. I used to share food with those who needed it. My friends would tease me, "How are you so selfless?" I'd laugh and say, "It's not selflessness, it's the biggest selfish act I do!" Because giving fills my soul with joy and blessings, more than any gold or fancy thing ever could. Like Denzel Washington said, "The most selfish thing you can do is help someone else. The joy it gives you? Nothing beats it." So don't be shy to be selfish like that. It's the only kind of selfishness Grandma approves.

The blessings of a hungry person? Don't underestimate them, they're like magic, I'm telling you. They can work miracles, faster than you can say "chicken curry." Even when you're rushing around, stop for a moment when you see someone struggling. Give what you can a little food, a kind word, a smile. The value of your gift isn't in its size, but in the heart that receives it. A small piece of bread for you is a feast for another. Thousands die every day because they don't have these simple things. That's a tragedy we can't afford to ignore.

Every time I give 10 when I only have 20, I find my blessings multiply, like magic filling my bag with 200. Life means nothing if we hoard all we have. Someone nearby might be suffering, from hunger, loneliness, or even just the absence of a kind word. If we let people die from these things, then what's the point of living? We fail not just them, but ourselves. Your ten rupees can save a life. Your words can save a mind from breaking. Your smile might be the only sunshine someone sees today. Your hug can heal a lonely heart. When you give with love, nothing is wasted. Only the one who receives knows the true value.

Let me tell you about a young girl I know. She was terrified of speaking on stage, as if the whole world would swallow her up. But she kept trying, every chance she got. After every performance, she longed to hear just one kind word, a little pat on the back , "You did great." She needed that like breath. Some people say, "Just believe in yourself, you don't need others' approval." But when you've been made to feel small for too long, a little kindness from others lights a fire inside you.

Imagine being in deep darkness, hoping someone says, "Keep going, you're on the right path." You can either laugh at their mistakes, pushing them back into the shadows, or you can say, "Hey, you did great up there! Just a couple of tweaks, but wow!" That little encouragement can be the difference between giving up or standing tall tomorrow.

Words have power, my dear. Proverbs 18:21 says, "Death and life are in the power of the tongue." I saw her friends mock her, not knowing their words were like tiny knives. She nearly broke. But then, one brave classmate said, "You rocked! A few fixes, but amazing!" Her face lit up like the first morning sun. I told her, "You were born for the stage," and she almost cried but those were tears of light, not darkness.

We all need a little validation sometimes. What you say can build someone up or tear them down. Reflect all the goodness you have inside it comes back to you in ways you never dreamed. Goodness spreads from one heart to another like ripples in a pond. That's how the world gets better, one small kindness at a time. So, live well, dear. Don't hold back goodness when you have the chance to give. You are truly rich when you share what someone else desperately needs.

The Science and Theories Behind Giving: Why Kindness Brings Abundance

Giving isn't just a nice idea Grandma talks about, science shows it's actually good for your brain, body, and life! When you give, you tap into some powerful psychological and biological mechanisms that create a cycle of abundance.

1. The "Helper's High" - How Giving Feels Good

When you help someone, your brain releases chemicals like dopamine and oxytocin, the same "feel-good" molecules that activate when you eat delicious food or receive love. This creates a sensation called the helper's high, a natural high that makes you feel happy, calm, and fulfilled.

- Dopamine is linked to reward and pleasure.
- Oxytocin is called the "bonding hormone" and makes you feel connected and trusting.

This chemical cocktail motivates you to keep giving because your brain rewards you with joy every time.

2. The Law of Reciprocity: Give and Receive

A big part of why giving leads to abundance is based on a social rule called reciprocity when you give to others, they feel a natural urge to give back, creating a cycle of mutual support.

- This isn't always immediate or obvious. Sometimes the return is emotional, like gratitude, trust, or friendship.
- Sometimes it's practical, someone might help you later, share information, or open doors to opportunities.

By building strong social bonds through generosity, you create a network that supports you in return.

3. Positive Psychology and Abundance Mindset

Psychologists talk about an abundance mindset, the belief that there's plenty to go around. People with this mindset tend to give more because they don't fear losing what they have. Instead, they see giving as an investment that creates more value.

- This mindset contrasts with a scarcity mindset, which focuses on lack and fear.
- Studies show that generosity reinforces positive emotions and reduces stress, depression, and anxiety.

Giving boosts your sense of purpose and well being, which attracts more positivity into your life.

4. Biological Impact: Giving is Good for Your Health

Believe it or not, giving actually improves your physical health too:

- Research shows generous people have lower blood pressure.
- Giving reduces stress hormones like cortisol.
- It strengthens the immune system, helping you live longer and feel better.

All these health benefits add up, allowing you to be more productive and energetic, which in turn can increase your ability to create and receive abundance.

5. Economic and Social Theories: The Power of Sharing

From an economic perspective, giving can be seen as social investment. By helping others, you increase social capital the goodwill and cooperation available in your community.

- This social capital often translates into economic benefits, such as job referrals, business partnerships, and collaborative opportunities.
- The "Pay It Forward" concept shows how one act of kindness can ripple through many people, creating a chain of generosity and support.

6. Spiritual and Philosophical Views

Many spiritual traditions say giving breaks the cycle of ego and selfishness, allowing you to connect with something bigger than yourself, which brings peace, contentment, and yes, abundance.

- The idea that "what you give comes back multiplied" is found in many cultures and religions, echoing the scientific truths about reciprocity and emotional well-being.

Now listen here, sugar, if holding onto grudges could fill your belly, we'd all be sitting at the table stuffed by now! But kindness? Oh, that fills your soul, and it comes with free tea, warm smiles, and a whole lot of peace. So give, honey, or you'll be missing out on the best recipe for a happy heart.

Remember this: *'A generous person will prosper.'* That's from Proverbs, and you best believe it's true. And don't forget what Romans tells us: *'If your enemy's hungry, feed him; if he's thirsty, give him a drink.'* That's real strength, not weakness. The Good Book also says, *'Whoever is kind to the poor is lending to the Lord, and He'll pay you back for it.'* That's a promise sweeter than grandma's honey cake. And from the Quran, wisdom too: *'Those who spend their wealth day and night, openly or in secret, will have their reward with the Lord.'*

Your true greatness, darling, isn't in what you hold onto, but in what you give away. Alice Hocker said it best: *'Your greatness is not in what you have but what you give.'*

Winston Churchill chimed in too, reminding us: *'We make a living by what we get, but we make a life by what we give.'* Now, isn't that the truth?

And remember the wise Mother Teresa's words, honey: *'Love ain't about pity, and charity ain't about handouts, it's about love. So don't just toss money, reach out your hand instead.' That's the kind of giving that lights up the world. And Martin Luther King Jr., bless his soul, reminded us that 'Everybody can be great, 'cause anybody can serve. You don't need a fancy degree or perfect grammar, just a heart full of grace and a soul fueled by love.'

So here's the gospel, sweetheart , give like your joy depends on it, because it truly does. You want peace, you want happiness? Don't sit there waiting for a miracle or for that perfect moment to come knocking. Start handing out some love, kindness, and whatever little you've got, and watch your life change faster than a kettle boiling on a cold winter morning. And listen, if you're still sitting on your hands, clutching your blessings like they're your last paratha, well... I'm ready to pull out my wooden spoon and remind you: generosity ain't just some fluffy idea, it's how you survive this crazy dance called life. You give, you get. You share, you grow. You help, you heal. Simple math, baby!

So get to giving, or get left behind like last year's chutney. Because hoarding won't fill your heart, and bitterness won't fill your belly. But giving? Giving fills both. Now, go on make your soul richer than your wallet ever was.

Grandma's Easy Peasy Guide to Giving (No Fuss, Just Love)

1. **Start Small, Sweetie**
   No need to give the whole farm right away! Even a smile or a kind word is giving. Say "thank you" warmly, hold the door open, or share your chai , small things count big.

2. **Carry a Little Extra**
   Whenever you go out, tuck a few extra snacks, some change, or even a clean handkerchief in your purse or pocket. You never know who might need a tiny helping hand.

3. **Give Time Like It's Gold**
   Sometimes, all a person wants is a little ear to listen. Put down your phone, look them in the eye, and give your time. That's worth more than any gift wrapped in shiny paper.

4. **Share What You Love**
   Have a favorite recipe, book, or song? Pass it on! Sharing your joys multiplies them and spreads happiness like grandma's homemade sweets.

5. **Compliment Like You Mean It**

Spot someone doing something good? Tell them! A genuine "You did great!" or "That color looks amazing on you!" is a gift that lights up hearts.

6. **Help in Secret, if You Can**

Sneaky giving is the best kind. Drop a little note, pay for someone's tea anonymously, or leave a kind message on someone's car. It's like magic that makes the world a little sweeter.

7. **Practice Giving Daily**

Make giving a little habit, even if it's just being patient when someone's slow or forgiving a small irritation. Your heart will stretch, and you'll feel lighter.

8. **Don't Forget Yourself**

Giving isn't just outward. Be kind to your own self too. Treat yourself with the same love you give others you deserve it, honey.

The Life Practices – Foundations for a Fulfilled Life Daily choices that align the body, mind, and spirit.

XXIII

Gratitude, Baby: Grandma's Secret Spice

"Gratitude is a fruit of great cultivation; you do not find it among gross people." – Samuel Johnson

Now listen here, sugar count your blessings before you start counting your problems, or you'll never know how rich you already are. Let's sit ourselves down and talk about one of life's greatest, most underrated superpowers: gratitude. Now, don't roll your eyes. I know you've probably heard folks yammer on about being thankful, like it's just some Pinterest quote you slap on your fridge next to expired coupons. But this ain't fluff. This is realnlife soul saving stuff.

You know that old line, *"I had the blues because I had no shoes, until I saw a man with no feet"*? We've all heard it, maybe even recited it. But did we really let it sink into our bones? See, the point is: we get so busy crying over the shoes we don't have, we forget to count the legs we're standing on. Perspective, darling, that's where the power is. Doris Day (bless her talented soul) once said, *"Gratitude is riches. Complaint is poverty."* And ain't that the gospel truth? You could be surrounded by diamonds and still feel poor if all you do is complain. Let me tell you something: someone out there is praying for the very life you're living right now. Yes, *your* life, with the cracked phone screen, chaotic mornings, and lukewarm coffee. Someone would trade you places in a heartbeat.

See, it's human nature to always want more. More success, more love, more likes, more whatever. And listen, wanting more? That's not a crime.

But baby, if you're not grateful for what you've got now, that "more" ain't never gonna feel like enough. You'll be chasing happiness like it's the ice cream truck you just missed by ten seconds, out of breath and still empty handed. Gratitude is what grounds you. It's what keeps your joy from slipping through your fingers.

Now let's address the part nobody wants to talk about: sometimes you go out of your way for folks, and they don't even say thank you. I know, it stings. But as Shakespeare (a dramatic man, but wise) said, *"Expectation is the root of all heartache."* Don't let someone else's lack of manners steal your peace. You don't express gratitude for applause you do it because it lifts *your* spirit. It's a gift you give yourself. Gratitude ain't always natural, especially if you've been through tough times, or you've been surrounded by folks who confuse complaining with conversation. But here's the thing: being grateful is a choice. A practice. A daily workout for your heart. And let me tell you, sweetpea, grateful hearts? They glow from the inside out.

Practicing gratitude doesn't just make you happier, it makes you healthier. And no, I'm not just talking about unicorn vibes and good juju. I'm talking about real, medical grade peace of mind. Studies back it up, but grandma's been preaching it for years: grateful folks sleep better, smile more, and cuss less (well, *slightly* less). Let me share one of my favorite stories. Imagine you're climbing a mountain. Halfway up, you realize you forgot your water bottle. You're thirsty, cranky, ready to throw in the towel. Then someone from the group hands you some water. You thank them and keep climbing. Later, you're ready to give up again, but someone offers hope. When you're about to collapse, someone offers a hand. Someone shares their food.

Now, when you finally reach that mountain top hair a mess, legs shaking you're looking at the view and thinking, *"Wow, I made it."* But pause, darling. Don't you dare forget those little acts of kindness that carried you when you couldn't carry yourself. Those hands, those voices, those moments *they* got you here. No matter how high you rise, don't forget the roots. Remember the ones who passed the water, the hope, the strength.

Even the good Lord Himself said in the Bible, *"Ask, and you shall receive; seek, and you shall find; knock, and the door shall be opened."* But don't you go bustin' through that door like you own the place and forget to say thank you! When you get what you prayed for, don't get amnesia, sugar. Gratitude is how you say, "I remember. I'm humbled. I'm blessed."

And don't just be thankful for the sparkly, sugar-coated stuff, be grateful for your past too. Joel Osteen put it plain and pretty: *"You are not defined by your past; you are prepared by your past."* That heartbreak? That failure? That mistake that makes you cringe in the shower? Baby, that was training. It made you stronger. Wiser. Softer in the right places and tougher in others. Don't waste time wishing the past was different. That's like tryin' to re-cook soup that's already been served. Instead, bless it and thank it, and keep on moving forward.

Now let's get real practical. Gratitude ain't just a feeling, it's a habit. And like any good habit, brushing your teeth, taking your vitamins, blocking your ex you gotta *practice* it daily.

The Science Behind Gratitude: Why It Works Like Soul Medicine

Now listen here, sugar, gratitude isn't just some fluffy feel good trend cooked up by self help books and Instagram quotes. No baby. It's backed by cold, hard science, and your old granny's heart knew it long before the lab coats did. When you practice gratitude, your brain responds like it's just received a warm hug from the universe.

1. Dopamine & Serotonin: Your Brain's Happy Juice

Gratitude triggers the release of *dopamine* and *serotonin*, the feel-good neurotransmitters that make you feel lighter, brighter, and more content. Think of them like the warm chocolate cake with ice-cream of brain chemicals comforting, mood lifting, and oh-so-satisfying. The more often you practice gratitude, the easier it becomes for your brain to release these mood-boosting chemicals. Over time, it rewires itself to look for the good.

2. Neuroplasticity: Rewiring That Noggin

Your brain, darling, is like a garden. Whatever you water grows. Practicing gratitude regularly strengthens neural pathways that focus on positive thinking and emotional regulation. This beautiful trick of the brain is called **neuroplasticity**, the ability of your mind to reshape itself based on where you place your attention. You think grateful thoughts often enough, and soon that becomes your brain's *default setting*. Imagine that living on autopilot, but your autopilot is peace.

3. Stress Reduction & Cortisol Control

Ever notice how angry, bitter people always look like they've been chewing lemons all their lives? That's cortisol working overtime. Gratitude, on the other hand, **lowers cortisol**, the stress hormone, helping you feel calmer and more in control. It's like putting your inner chaos on a rocking chair with a cup of tea peaceful, grounded, and unbothered.

4. Better Sleep, Healthier Heart, Stronger Relationships

Multiple studies, including research published in *The Journal of Psychosomatic Research*, have shown that people who practice gratitude sleep better, have fewer aches and pains, and even enjoy lower blood pressure. Plus, they tend to have deeper relationships because when you're thankful, you're also more empathetic, less aggressive, and way more pleasant to be around. And let's be honest, nobody wants to cuddle up next to a chronic complainer.

5. Gratitude Reduces Toxic Emotions

Dr. Robert Emmons, one of the leading scientific experts on gratitude, found in his research that gratitude **blocks toxic emotions** like envy, resentment, and regret. You simply can't hold deep gratitude and soul-souring bitterness in your heart at the same time. One kicks the other out. (Kind of like when I shooed that cow away from my tulsi pot, one of us had to go, and it wasn't gonna be me!)

Here's how to get started:

Start Each Day with Gratitude:

Spend 5–10 minutes every morning writing down what you're thankful for. Can't think of anything? Start with the basics air in your lungs, light in your room, coffee in your cup. Write one thing instead of 5. Ask yourself: *What would life be like without this?* Sit with that thought. Let it humble you. Let it soften you. Gratitude is like a muscle the more you flex it, the stronger it gets. Every breath is a blessing, baby.

Say "Thank You" Louder:

"Thank you" isn't just polite, it's powerful. It resets your spirit. Say it more often, and mean it. Thank the barista. Thank your mama. Thank God. Thank who made you smile. Say it like you're sprinkling holy glitter on your day. And remember: the people who roll their eyes at thank you's and sorry's? They're usually the ones who need a little humble pie.

Share Your Gratitude:

If someone made you smile *tell them.* Don't hoard your appreciation like it's the last piece of chocolate. Gratitude grows when you pass it on. Write that note. Send that message. Speak that compliment. What you put out into the world comes back, sugar. You don't just get what you want, you get what you *give.*

Practicing gratitude doesn't just change your mood, it changes your life. It doesn't mean ignoring your pain or pretending everything's perfect. It means choosing to see the light even on the cloudy days. And when you make gratitude a habit? Oh, honey you won't need luck. You'll have joy.

So don't wait for a perfect life to be thankful. Be thankful, and you'll see just how beautiful life already is.

Listen here, sweetplum! Your brain? It's like an old radio that can pick up all kinds of static complaints, worries, fears. But gratitude? Gratitude is the dial that tunes you into a higher frequency. The one where love, peace, and perspective live. You get to choose: listen to that endless noise, or switch over to the station that feeds your soul.

And don't come at me with, "But I'm wired for worry!" Listen here, honey, practicing gratitude is like when you clean out that junk drawer in the kitchen. At first, it's a hot mess: random spoons, old receipts, half used packets of something you don't even remember buying. But once you take a minute to sort through it, toss the trash, and find those forgotten treasures, suddenly the whole drawer feels lighter, cleaner, and ready for what really matters.

That's gratitude for your mind, a good declutter that makes room for the sweet stuff. So don't be scared to toss out the grumbles and complaints crowding your thoughts. Clear them out, and watch how much brighter your whole day feels.Gratitude is your reset button, baby. Hit it hard, hit it often.

Every sacred text worth its salt says the same thing. The Bible says, "In all things give thanks." Not just the easy stuff, not just when the chai's hot, but all of it. The Quran promises, "If you give thanks, I will give you more." More blessings, more strength, more light. The Bhagavad Gita? It says God accepts anything you offer with a pure heart, a leaf, a flower, a sip of water and you better believe that counts.

Cicero, that wise old Roman, said gratitude is the mother of all virtues. And Rumi? That soul said, "Gratitude is wine for the soul. Go on, get drunk." So don't hold back drink it in deep. Amy Collette put it like this: gratitude sparks a fire of joy inside your soul. And Mary Davis? She nailed it: "The more grateful I am, the more beauty I see." And it's true. When you're grateful, even the cracked tiles and faded curtains start looking like a masterpiece.

So listen, darling, don't go chasing happiness like it's some far off treasure. It's already in your hands, wrapped up in the everyday. The roof over your head, the food on your plate, even those hard lessons that shaped you say thank you for all of it. Because gratitude isn't just a feeling, it's a way of living. Make it your habit. Make it your power. Let it pour out of you like sweet cardamom in a hot cup of chai. That's where your peace is hiding. Find it, hold it tight, and never let it go.

XXIV
Spend Time with Nature

"By discovering nature, you discover yourself."-Maxime Lagace

Grandma always says, *"If life feels noisy, go listen to the trees,they're quieter, but far wiser."* Man's greatest lessons and most profound awakenings often come not from books, but from the birdsong at dawn, the steady hum of the wind, and the gentle dance of sunlight on water. Nature has forever been our oldest teacher. Long before schools and screens, man learned from the rustling leaves, the rising sun, and the changing seasons.

Across cultures, this truth is echoed. Buddha found enlightenment not in a palace, but under a tree. In Hindu philosophy, the *Panchabhuta*, earth, water, fire, air, and ether aren't just elements, they're living scriptures. Each one whispers timeless truths about balance, humility, and the art of simply *being*. If you can't hear what your soul is saying, go outside it's always louder there.

The Universe in Every Leaf

There's nothing that nature cannot teach us. The tiniest pebble has known pressure, time, and change(every pebble is a result of the pressure it has endured- pebbles get their shape from being knocked around, kind of like people, darling.). The vast ocean teaches surrender through its tides, the mountain teaches stillness through its silence, and the seed teaches faith through its quiet, unseen growth.Nature isn't just here to help us survive, it's here to help us *remember*. Remember joy. Stillness. Wonder. The city may build ambition, but the forest? It builds peace.

A man who spends his morning beside a river, his feet in the soil and his mind among the clouds, often feels a happiness a metropolitan heart may never know. There's a saying Grandma loved: *A walk in nature walks the soul back home.*

And isn't that the truth? Nature brings us back to ourselves.

The Universality of Nature's Lessons

What makes nature's wisdom extraordinary is its universality. The sun shines on the saint and the sinner alike. The rain falls on broken rooftops and blooming roses without discrimination. The same mountain might look like strength to one person and solitude to another. Grandma would chuckle and say, *God didn't hang signs on trees to tell you what they mean. He left it for your soul to figure out.*

Spending time in nature isn't just a break, it's a gentle schooling, a sacred therapy, and sometimes, a divine intervention. You don't need to live in a cabin or meditate by a lake to feel it. Just step out, even for ten minutes. Let the wind comb through your thoughts. Let the earth remind you that you're grounded. In that stillness, you won't just find answers, you'll find better questions.

"In every walk with nature, one receives far more than he seeks."- John Muir

Lessons from Nature: My Takeaways

1. The Sun: Consistency Is Strength

Even when hidden by clouds, the sun rises and sets, every single day. That unwavering rhythm taught me the power of simply *showing up*. Life won't always be bright, but like the sun, we must still rise.

"The moment you take responsibility for everything in your life is the moment you can change anything."- Hal Elrod

Let the sun remind us: consistency isn't boring, it's holy.

2. Weeds – The Hidden Purpose of Struggles

To most, weeds are nuisances, something to be pulled out. But Grandma would say, *"Even weeds know how to survive storms. Can you say the same?"* In truth, weeds hold the soil together, prevent erosion, and enrich it when they decompose.

Life's weeds, our discomfort, loss, or setbacks often strengthen us quietly. They prepare the soil of our soul for stronger roots and richer growth. They're not problems; they're part of the process.

3. Water – Adaptability Is Power

Water is soft and yielding, yet it wears down the hardest rock. It changes shape but never loses its essence. From rivers to rain, water teaches the power of graceful adaptability.

"Be water, my friend."– Bruce Lee

When life asks us to shift, flow, or bend, may we remember the quiet power in staying true while staying flexible.

4. Trees – Rooted Resilience

Trees don't run from storms. They endure, deeply rooted, swaying but rarely snapping. They remind us that our hidden inner work our values, relationships, and self-discipline, is what keeps us grounded.

"A tree with strong roots laughs at storms."

Even as we grow, rise, and stretch ourselves toward the sky, let's never forget to stay rooted in humility. Grandma would say, *"No matter how far you rise, keep your roots soaked in gratitude."*

5. The Moon – Light in Every Darkness

The moon doesn't always shine in full. Sometimes it's barely a sliver, but it still shows up. The moon taught me that we're allowed to be incomplete, imperfect, or healing, and still offer light.

"Courage doesn't always roar. Sometimes it's the quiet voice at the end of the day whispering, 'I will try again tomorrow.'"- Mary Anne Radmacher

Like the moon, even in our lowest phases, we can still show up. Small light is still light.

6. The Clouds: Embrace Impermanence

Clouds drift and change without clinging. They teach us that everything in life, people, pain, joy is fleeting. What stays is the sky within us.

"Try not to resist the changes that come your way... How do you know that the side you are used to is better than the one to come?"- Rumi

Let's learn to flow with change, to grieve what's gone, but also to look up and welcome what's next.

7. The Caterpillar: Never Underestimate Growth

Now listen, child, nobody claps for the caterpillar. Folks only show up when the wings come out. But Grandma would say, *"Don't you dare judge your journey while you're still in the cocoon."* That squishy little thing? It's cooking up something glorious. And so are you. Don't rush it. Just because people can't see your potential doesn't mean God forgot it.

"Just when the caterpillar thought the world was over, it became a butterfly."- *Barbara Haines Howett*

So hush that panic voice in your head. Trust the mess. Trust the silence. Trust your transformation.

8.The Waves: Keep Moving Forward

Life will smack you like a wave, again and again. But baby, even the ocean never quits. Grandma used to say, *"If the waves can keep crashing and still look that pretty, so can you.*" Get knocked down? Fine. Just don't unpack there.

"Out of suffering have emerged the strongest souls; the most massive characters are seared with scars." – Kahlil Gibran

You were made to rise, not rust. Keep moving, no matter how many times life tries to drag you under.

9.Flowers: Live Fully, No Matter How Brief

A flower doesn't ask how long it'll live. It just blooms. Boldly. Brightly. And it gives what it has while it can. Grandma would point a marigold and say, *"This tiny thing does more for the world in five days than some folks do in fifty years."*

"What is the essence of life? To serve others and to do good." – Aristotle

So bloom. Love loud. Serve sweet. Your impact ain't measured in years, it's measured in how you made people feel.

10.Rainbows: Be Someone's Light

Storms happen. That's just weather being dramatic. But a rainbow? That's heaven saying, *"Hey, I'm still here."*

Grandma would look out after a storm and sigh, *"Be someone's rainbow, child. The world's cloudy enough."*

"Try to be a rainbow in someone's cloud." - Maya Angelou

You don't have to fix the whole world. Just brighten a corner of it.

11.The Spider: Persevere Through Failure

Oh honey, Grandma loves a spider. She'd say, *"That eight legged genius builds a house with no hands. And when it breaks? It builds again."* You mess up? So what. Try again. Fall again? Get up, again.

"Do not judge me by my success; judge me by how many times I fell down and got back up again." – Nelson Mandela

Life's not about getting it perfect. It's about refusing to quit.

12. The Hilltop View: Perspective on Insignificance

Climb a hill, child. Look out over the world, and suddenly that thing you were crying about? It's the size of an ant's eyelash.

Grandma would say, *"You ain't the center of the universe, sugar, so stop acting like it."*

"Look deep into nature, and then you will understand everything better." – Albert Einstein

Let the vastness humble you. Life's too short to carry every worry like a purse.

13. The Road Not Taken: Follow Your Own Path

Robert Frost had it right, and Grandma backed him up: *"Just 'cause everyone's*

walking one way doesn't mean it's not dumb."
You've got your own road. Take it. Even if it's bumpy and no one's clapping. Especially then.

"Two roads diverged in a wood, and I, I took the one less traveled by, and that has made all the difference."

You ain't here to copy. You're here to carve. But if you believe in the common road unapologetically take that, never make a choice to just ma

The Science: Nature Doesn't Hurry, Yet Everything Gets Done

Look closely at how the seasons shift, how rivers shape mountains, or how seeds push through soil. These aren't random acts they follow biological laws and rhythms we humans are *also* wired to obey.

- Circadian rhythms run our body clocks, just like the sun commands day and night.
- Neuroplasticity in the brain mimics how forests adapt after fire neurons reroute, regrow, and heal.
- Ecosystems teach interdependence. No creature thrives alone. Neither do we.

Grandma would say: "You ever seen a tree grow overnight? Nope. But every morning it's a little taller. Same goes for your peace and purpose, baby."

The Theory: Transformation Is Nature's Default Mode

We tend to think change is hard. Nature thinks otherwise.

- Entropy and Renewal: Physics says everything moves toward chaos, unless it renews itself. Nature doesn't resist change; it *requires* it.
- Cycles Over Timelines: Nature doesn't run by deadlines, it flows in cycles. Like the moon, like the tides, like your healing. Some days you'll shine, other days you'll retreat. Both are sacred.
- Non linear Progress: A seed doesn't grow in a straight line. It breaks, roots, waits, stretches, and only then blooms. Why should your journey be any simpler?

Grandma would grin and say: "Child, even the moon takes its sweet time to become full. Don't rush what's meant to unfold."

All the lessons you need? They're not in some self help seminar. They're out there, woven into spiderwebs, blooming on branches, whispered by the wind. Grandma would always say, *"God gave you nature before He gave you Google don't act like you know better."*

Even the best inventions we've made airplanes, art, architecture, are just nature's ideas we copied. And the smallest things? They've got the biggest wisdom. A falling leaf doesn't cry. It just lets go and trusts the next season. That, right there, is divine intelligence. Learn it.

"Adopt the pace of nature: her secret is patience." – *Ralph Waldo Emerson*

So go outside. Really. Take your tangled thoughts, your broken heart, your tired feet and walk. Listen. Let the wind sort out your nonsense. Let the trees remind you how to stay still. Let the birds teach you to sing again. Nature's not just pretty. She's powerful. And she's waiting for you to pay attention. Grandma would say, *"Child, stop scrolling and start strolling. The earth's been holding answers longer than you've been alive."*

"In every walk with nature, one receives far more than he seeks." – *John Muir*

Practical Steps to Connect Deeply with Nature

1. **Make Nature a Daily Habit:**
   Even if it's just 10–15 minutes, step outside every day, whether it's your backyard, a park, or just a tree-lined street. Consistency builds connection.

2. **Observe Mindfully:**
   Slow down and really notice the details: the rustle of leaves, the way the sunlight filters through branches, the patterns on a flower or the shape of a pebble. Use all your senses, sight, sound, smell, touch.

3. **Practice Grounding:**
   Take off your shoes and feel the earth beneath your feet. Feel the solid support of the ground, and breathe deeply to center yourself.

4. **Journal Your Observations and Insights:**
   Write down what you noticed or felt during your time outdoors. Reflect on any lessons or emotions that came up, like patience from watching a growing tree or resilience from watching waves crash.

5. **Use Nature as a Meditation Guide:**
   Focus on natural rhythms like your breathing synced with the wind, or the steady sway of branches. Let these rhythms calm your mind and bring you into the present moment.

6. **Bring Nature Indoors:**
   Keep plants, flowers, or even natural objects like stones or shells in your living space. Touch or look at them to remind yourself of nature's lessons

throughout the day.

7. **Embrace the Seasons:**
Notice the changes through the year, buds in spring, full blooms in summer, falling leaves in autumn, bare branches in winter. Reflect on how change is natural and necessary for growth.

8. **Practice Letting Go Like a Leaf:**
When facing stress or difficulty, visualize yourself as a leaf gently falling and letting go. Trust the natural cycle of release and renewal.

9. **Seek Quiet and Stillness:**
Find a quiet spot outdoors and simply sit or lie down, allowing yourself to be still and absorb the calmness around you.

XXV

The Power of Words- What You Say Can Save a Life

"Be careful with your words. Once they are said, they can only be forgiven, not forgotten."

Sweetheart, let me sit you down and tell you something your generation(mine more than yours but most of us or already dead) needs to tattoo on their hearts: your words carry weight, real, soul crushing or soul lifting weight.

You don't need a sword to break someone, just one careless word can do it. I've seen it, sugar: one sharp comment, one cruel joke, and a soul hanging by a thread can quietly fall apart. Now, I'm not trying to guilt you. I'm trying to *wake you up*. Because here's the truth: everyone is fighting something you can't see. That loud girl at the party? She cries herself to sleep. That quiet boy in the corner? He's wondering if he matters to anyone at all. And sometimes, all it takes is a gentle, kind word to remind someone they're still seen. Still wanted. Still enough.

I once told a girl who looked like she was going to disappear , "You have the kind of eyes that hold galaxies. Don't dim them for anyone." She cried. Said no one had ever spoken to her like that. Not once. Can you imagine that? In a world full of mouths, she'd never heard kindness meant for her. That's the magic you hold. A kind word is a free miracle. So why not give them out like laddus on Diwali?

And don't get it twisted, this isn't about being fake or soft. Grandma doesn't do fake. This is about being *intentional*. Being the kind of person who *pauses before you pounce.*

Like I always say, "If you wouldn't tattoo it on someone's soul, maybe don't say it at all."

So here's your reminder:

Speak life.

Speak love.

Speak light.

Because what you say might just be the thing that keeps someone breathing another day.

"Kind words can be short and easy to speak, but their echoes are truly endless." – Mother Teresa . Use your voice, baby. But use it like a lighthouse, not a matchstick.

Words Can Build or Break

"The tongue has the power of life and death." – Proverbs 18:21

Sweetheart, let Grandma tell you something she learned the hard way: You don't need fists to bruise someone. You don't need a weapon to leave scars. A sharp tongue will do just fine.

Words? They're like spells. One sentence can either lift a soul from the dirt or shove it six feet under. I've seen both.

For 15 years, I was scared of my own voice. No kidding. I'd sit in the back, hiding behind my hair, hoping no one would call on me. I'd rehearse "here" during roll call like I was auditioning for a Broadway play. That's how nervous I was.Then came the day I had to speak on stage, I thought my knees would quit before I got to the mic. But there she was, Professor Brinda, sitting in the front row, smiling like I was Maya Angelou herself. She didn't just listen. She believed in me. And when I finished, she said,"Sniffa, it's like you were born for the stage. You owned it."

Baby, that one line, that one kind sentence replaced *years* of fear and silence. I stood a little taller after that. I've never looked back.Now imagine if she'd said,"That wasn't clear."or "You should've stayed quiet." Oh honey, I would've folded and never spoken again.

That's how powerful words are.

You never know who's barely holding it together. That barista who got your name wrong? Might be battling a heartbreak. That kid in class who talks too much? Might be silencing pain. So choose kindness, not perfection. Studies show kindness literally rewires the brain, it raises serotonin, reduces stress, and strengthens trust. And not just for the one receiving, but for the one *giving* it too. Science backs what Grandma always said: "Speak life, or don't speak at all." You don't have to fix someone's world. Just don't be the reason they feel broken in it. One kind word can rewrite someone's story , just like Brinda rewrote mine. And remember this, darling: "People may forget what you said, but they will never forget how you made them feel." – Maya Angelou So go ahead, compliment the stranger. Your words might just be the thing that keeps someone standing.

Speak Like Every Word Matters- Because It Does

"Let your conversation be always full of grace, seasoned with salt." – *Colossians 4:6*

Now listen, sugar. Grandma's got no time for people who spit fire just to feel powerful. Saying "I'm just being real" ain't an excuse to be rude. That's not honesty, that's immaturity in a glittery hat. Real strength? Real grace? It's knowing when to speak and how to speak, with love, not ego. I always ask myself before opening my mouth: "Will this lift someone up? Or weigh them down?"

If it doesn't add light, I zip it like I'm locking away my good jewellery during a house party.

You see, I've made a quiet promise with my tongue: No breaking hearts. No belittling dreams. Even when I'm correcting someone, I serve it warm, like a bowl of soup, seasoned, not scalding. And Lord knows I've seen people confuse loudness with boldness. But hear me when I say: "Thunder makes noise. Rain grows flowers." – Rumi

Wanna be bold? Be kind. Speak truth? Speak it gently. Because honey, if you've got something to say, make sure it's worth hearing.

Even Gandhi said it best: "Speak only if it improves upon the silence." And Grandma agrees. Silence is golden, don't trade it for rust.

Remember that time I overheard a teenage girl whispering she wanted to disappear because someone told her she wasn't pretty enough? I sat beside her, looked her in the eyes, and said,

"Baby, the world's got enough mirrors. What it needs is more light, and you are a whole sunrise." That girl smiled through her tears and said no one had ever spoken to her like that. One kind word. That's all it took.

"Words are free. It's how you use them that may cost you." – Kipling
Use yours to build, not bruise. So darling, next time you're tempted to "tell it like it is," ask yourself: Is it true? Is it kind? Is it necessary?
And if it ain't all three, well then, bless their heart and hush.

Because in this loud, chaotic world, the real power is in graceful speech and a strong heart.

Say No to Gossip, Say Yes to Growth

Now listen up, sweetheart. If there's one habit that'll age your soul and wrinkle your spirit faster than smoking and sun damage combined, it's gossip. That ugly little pastime dressed up as "just talking" is poison in a teacup. And I say this with love: sip something better.

I used to fall for it, too. I'd listen, nod, add a little spice, maybe even throw in a dramatic "really?" like I wasn't stirring the pot myself. And Lord, don't get me started on how many times I was the *main course* on someone else's gossip menu.

But the day I started walking closer with God, something shifted. Peace started costing too much to waste on pettiness."*Do not let any unwholesome talk come out of your mouths, but only what is helpful for building others up."* – *Ephesians 4:29*

That verse right there? It slapped me awake harder than Auntie Munima's sandal.

Now, if you eavesdrop on my conversations, darling, you'll only hear names mentioned when I'm lifting someone up. Because here's the truth: talking down about others doesn't make you taller. And I've got better things to do than chew on someone else's reputation. Like growing. Healing. Drinking my tea, not spilling it.

"Great minds discuss ideas. Average minds discuss events. Small minds discuss people." -Eleanor Roosevelt

And baby, I wasn't born to be small-minded. Neither were you.

Every minute you spend dragging someone's name is a minute you could've spent building your own. Gossip robs you of integrity, joy, even blessings. You're speaking negativity into the world, and trust me, it circles back.

"Whoever gossips to you will gossip about you." – *Spanish Proverb*
True as daylight.

Want to glow different? Shut down that gossip chain. Switch the subject. Refuse to entertain it. And if someone insists? Smile, sip your tea, and say, "If we're not helping them, let's not talk about them." Protect your peace like your Grandma protects her young boyfriend from evil eyes fiercely. Because your words are either building bridges or burning them. And love, bridges take longer to build than they do to destroy.

So next time gossip comes knocking, don't answer the door. Growth lives here. And she doesn't have time for nonsense.

The Words You Tell Yourself

Now sugar, let Grandma sit you down for a minute and tell you something real important:

What you say to yourself when no one's watching? That's what shapes your destiny.

You could be dressed , praised by the world, with a thousand likes on your Instagram, but if your own mind is whispering "I'm not enough," you'll feel empty no matter how loud the applause is. And baby, I've been there. I've stood in front of the mirror and heard voices that weren't God's , but voices of fear, shame, insecurity, and lies.

"As a man thinks in his heart, so is he." – Proverbs 23:7

That's not just scripture, honey. That's your soul's blueprint. You see, the most important conversation you'll ever have is the one you're having inside your own head.

If you keep repeating,

- "I'm too late,"
- "I'm not smart enough,"
- "I always mess things up"…
  then don't be surprised when your life starts to follow those scripts like a badly written soap opera.
- But if you flip the script? Oh honey, watch heaven move.

Start declaring, even when you don't feel it yet:

- "I am enough."
- "I am growing, not behind."
- "I am chosen, not overlooked."
- "I am healing, not broken."

Because let me tell you, God doesn't speak in insults. He doesn't label you with your past. He calls you redeemed, loved, a masterpiece in progress. Who are you to argue with the Artist?

"You are what you believe." – Oprah Winfrey

"Your words become your world." – Nido Qubein

So darling, cancel the lies. Fire the inner critic. Hire a new narrator, one that speaks like your Creator does. One that sees your potential even on your worst day.

And here's Grandma's golden rule:

Don't you dare say something to yourself that you wouldn't say to a child you love. Speak to yourself like someone worth rooting for, because you are.

"Kind words can be short and easy to speak, but their echoes are truly endless."
– Mother Teresa

So go ahead. Speak light. Speak life. Speak love. Because when your words change, your life does too.

No Bad Words – A Clean Mouth, A Clear Mind

Now baby, I know this might sound old-fashioned in a world where people cuss like it's seasoning in every sentence, but hear me out: Choosing clean words changes everything.

Not just how people see you but how you see you.

You see, every word you speak is either adding poison or planting peace. When you toss around harsh, vulgar, or angry words, even "just for fun" they leave a residue. They clutter your mind, tighten your chest, and before you know it, your inner world starts to match your outer language: chaotic, sharp, restless.

"Clean language cultivates clean thoughts. Clean thoughts create a peaceful heart."

Grandma always says, "You don't need to curse to sound powerful. You need truth, not volume."

There was a time I thought swearing made me tough, like it gave my pain a punchline. But the truth? It only made me feel more bitter, more reactive, more small. When I stopped cussing, I didn't just clean up my speech I calmed my spirit. I started choosing words that built bridges instead of burning them.

"Raise your words, not your voice. It is rain that grows flowers, not thunder." – Rumi

"What comes out of your mouth is what is in your heart." – Luke 6:45

It's not about pretending to be perfect, sugar. It's about choosing to be intentional.

When your language gets gentler, your life gets gentler. When your mouth stops spewing fire, your soul stops living in smoke.

I began to notice something else too:

- I thought before I reacted.
- I didn't need to shout to be heard.
- I could sit in silence without exploding.
- I started speaking life and baby, that *felt* like power.

And don't let anyone tell you soft words are weak. It takes real strength to stay kind when the world is cruel. It takes discipline to be calm when chaos is trending.

"Words are free. It's how you use them that may cost you." – KushandWizdom

So here's the grandma truth: You don't need profanity to be passionate. You don't need to swear to stand up for yourself. You don't need to shout to matter. Speak like someone who knows their words carry weight, because they do.

Keep it clean, keep it kind, keep it powerful.

The Emotional Contagion Theory-Your Words Influence More Than You Know

Now listen here, sugar, this Emotional Contagion Theory is no joke. It means that feelings spread from one person to another, mostly through the words we say, the tone we use, and even our facial expressions. Psychologists have proven this, your mood is kind of like a virus, but thankfully, it can be a *good* one when you use kind and loving words.

When you speak with warmth and encouragement, you're passing around what scientists call "positive emotional contagion." It's like throwing a pebble in a pond, those ripples reach everyone nearby, whether it's your family, friends, or coworkers. And studies show that when leaders talk positively, their whole team lifts up, works better, and feels happier. But if the words are harsh or negative, well, that bad mood spreads just as fast and can drag everyone down.

Let me give you a story, honey. Picture Grandma's kitchen on a Sunday afternoon. I'm chopping onions and humming a tune, telling stories that make everyone laugh. Even Cousin Joe, who came in grumbling, starts cracking a smile. By the time the stew is simmering, the whole family's sitting around the table, lighter in spirit and sharing hugs. That warmth isn't just from the stove it's the power of emotional contagion. My kind words and good mood caught like wildfire, lifting the whole house.

So remember, baby, your words are more powerful than you think. When you choose kindness, you don't just help one person — you change the energy of everyone around you. That's the science and the Grandma magic all wrapped up.

Daily Habits to Keep Your Tongue Sweet

1. Bless Before You Blast

   Before you open that mouth of yours, ask yourself: "Will this build someone up or tear them down?" If it ain't kind, don't say. Grandma always says, "If your words can't bloom, let 'em stay buried."

2. Start the Day Speaking Life

   Look in the mirror and say something loving, even if your hair's looking like a wild bird's nest. Say:"I am grateful to have hair."

3. Compliment Like You Mean It

   If someone's rocking a new haircut or just glowing with joy, tell them! Not just "Nice shirt," but "You look radiant in that color,!" Specific. Sincere. Spice it with sweetness.

4. Be mindful of Gossiping

   When you're tempted to gossip, vent, or say something snarky, chew gum, drink water, hum a hymn. Anything but spill poison. What you don't say is just as powerful as what you do.

5. Text Something Beautiful

   Once a day, send someone a kind message. Could be a "Thinking of you," a prayer, or a meme that makes them laugh. Small things warm hearts, baby. That's how you water friendships.

6. Turn Criticism into Construction

   Got feedback? Wrap it in honey. Instead of "You did it wrong," try, "Here's what might help next time." See? Same dish, just served on a better plate.

7. Say Thank You Like It's a Ritual

   Thank the cashier. Thank the bus driver. Thank your feet for carrying you. Gratitude is the softest language with the loudest impact.

8. Pray Before You Pop Off

   When someone's trying your last nerve, whisper a quick prayer: *"Lord, tame my tongue before I say something I'll need to repent for."* Works wonders. Saved Grandma many church apologies.

9. End the Day With a Soft Word

   Before bed, bless your day and bless someone else with a kind word. Say goodnight like it's the last thing they'll ever hear. Because love, one day, it will be.

10. Practice Saying Names with Honor
    Call people what lifts them: "champ," "love," "friend". Don't just say their names,speak their worth every time you do.

What you say can mean the difference between healing and hurting. Choose wisely." – Lisa Bevere

Words are sacred. They're not just sounds, they're seeds. Every sentence you speak takes root in someone's heart, and it will grow into something. You may forget what you said, but the one who received it won't. Your words could become the echo someone hears at their lowest, or the light that finally reaches their darkness.So speak life. Speak like your words are a lifeline because sometimes, they are.

Speak as if someone's breakthrough is waiting on the other side of your sentence, because it just might be.

And always remember:"If you can't find the right words, choose the kind ones."

In a world hungry for hope, be the voice that heals, not the noise that harms.

XXVI
The Power of Speed in Success

Child, if you wait for everything to be perfect, you'll be waiting forever, and your tea will be cold. That's exactly what grandma would say. Success doesn't come to those who sit around polishing their dreams like fine china. It comes to those who roll up their sleeves, burn the first batch of cookies, and still go back to bake again. The world doesn't reward those who dream the longest, it rewards those who act the fastest.

Tony Robbins put it perfectly: *"Success loves speed."* But let's be real, Grandma said it long before he did. Only she put it differently:
"You've got to get a move on, honey. Don't let life pass you by while you're still brushing your hair."

The Illusion of Perfection

Oh, perfection. That shiny, slippery idea we chase like a cat after a red dot. You think if you just plan more, learn more, wait a little longer, then maybe, *maybe* you'll be ready. But sweetheart, let me tell you something: perfection is a pretty lie that keeps you from starting.

Winston Churchill warned us: "Perfection is the enemy of progress." And grandma Sniffa says:
You don't need to have all your ducks in a row. Sometimes, you gotta start walking and let the ducks catch up.

The truth is, every person you admire, every leader, every innovator, every success story started messy. They made awkward first moves. They launched when they were scared. They didn't wait for permission. Because done is always better than perfect.

Learning Through Action

You don't get stronger by reading about lifting weights. You get stronger by *picking them up.*

Life works the same way. If you want to grow, you've got to get in the game, skin your knees a few times, and figure it out as you go. Thomas Edison didn't cry over his 10,000 failures. He saw them as steps. Each one got him closer to that lightbulb moment. Literally. Mistakes aren't proof you're failing. They're proof you're moving. And movement beats stillness every single day.

The Intuition Advantage

We live in a world drowning in advice, information, and "how to" guides. But sometimes, your heart whispers what Google can't.

Successful people? They listen to that whisper. They don't wait for every detail to be crystal clear. They trust their gut, take the leap, and adjust midair. Napoleon Hill said, "Don't wait. The time will never be just right." And grandma? "If it feels right in your bones, do it. And if it doesn't work, at least you'll have a story to tell."

Consistency Beats Perfection

Speed without consistency is like a firecracker, loud but over too fast. But speed with consistency? That's a roaring fire that warms a whole house.

When Grandma started *Chai and Conversation* with my friends in 2020, we were on fire, fast, passionate, full of ideas. But we fizzled out. Not because the dream wasn't good. Not because the vision wasn't big. But because we didn't keep showing up. We let the excitement fade, and with it, the progress. Looking back now, I can say this with love and truth: I sabotaged something great by slowing down when I should've kept going.

That's what inconsistency does, it quietly kills momentum.

And the lesson grandma learnt from this is that if you're going to start something, baby, see it through. Half-baked bread feeds no one.

Overcoming the Fear of Failure

Ah, fear. That sneaky little thief. It'll whisper, "What if you fail?"

But darling, let's flip the question: What if you *don't* start? What will you miss then?

Wayne Gretzky said, "You miss 100% of the shots you don't take." You won't learn to swim standing on the shore. Get in the water, even if it's deep.Failure isn't fatal. It's fertilizer. It grows your courage, thickens your skin, and deepens your wisdom.

The Winner's Mindset

Let's cut to it. Winners don't wait. They don't wait for applause, or approval, or a mood swing. They *start*. They *move*. They *try*.

They know that success doesn't come from knowing more, it comes from *doing* more.

Walt Disney said it best: "The way to get started is to quit talking and begin doing."

And your grandma says:"Stop yapping, start clapping, and get going already!"

In today's world, where everyone has access to the same internet, same apps, and same opportunities, the difference is not *what* you have, it's *how fast* you use it.

So here's your grandma style truth bomb, sweetie:

Stop overthinking. Stop planning your dream to death. Stop fearing the mess. Life is messy. Success is messy. You've just got to be the one who starts moving while everyone else is still ironing their shirts.Because a year from now, you'll either look back proud...Or wish you had started today.So what'll it be?

Psychology Behind Speed:

1. Zeigarnik Effect

This effect shows that our brain remembers unfinished tasks better than completed ones. When you start something quickly but don't finish it, your brain stays focused on it, creating a mental drive to complete the task. Starting fast helps build momentum and keeps your motivation alive because your mind wants to "close the loop."

2. Action Bias

Humans naturally prefer to act rather than stay still, especially when under pressure or stress. This tendency is called action bias. People who move quickly tap into this bias, avoiding paralysis by analysis, and making progress even when they don't have all the answers.

3. Dual-Process Theory (Neuroscience & Psychology)

Our brain has two systems of thinking:

- **System 1:** Fast, automatic, intuitive, and emotional. It's what helps us make quick decisions based on gut feelings.
- **System 2:** Slow, logical, and deliberate. This is where careful thinking and analysis happen.

Successful people learn to trust their fast System 1 thinking in the right moments so they can act quickly without getting stuck in overthinking.

4. Lean Startup Methodology

Popularized by Eric Ries, this method encourages launching a product or idea quickly, even if imperfect and then improving it based on real user feedback. It shows that speed helps you learn faster, adapt quickly, and avoid wasting time on perfecting something no one wants.

5. Perfectionism and Procrastination

Fear of making mistakes or not doing something perfectly often leads to procrastination and delay. Perfectionism becomes a trap. Moving fast helps you break out of this cycle by encouraging "good enough" decisions and learning through doing rather than waiting for perfect conditions.

6. Satisficing vs. Maximizing (Decision Theory)

- **Maximizers** try to find the absolute best choice and often get stuck weighing options.
- **Satisficers** make decisions that are good enough and move on quickly.

Fast movers act like satisficers they don't waste time hunting for perfection and avoid decision fatigue by deciding and acting swiftly.

7. Evolutionary Psychology: The Power of Quick Action

Our ancestors survived because they acted fast when faced with danger, they either fought or fled. This "fight or flight" instinct is hardwired into our brains. In today's world, this natural urge to respond quickly can be our greatest advantage. Those who move swiftly are more likely to seize opportunities, avoid pitfalls, and stay ahead in the race of life.

Practical Steps to Practice Speed

1. **Set Time Limits for Decisions**
   Give yourself a strict deadline to decide, like 3 minutes for small choices like the coffee choice or the place you want to eat, 1 day for bigger ones. This prevents overthinking and forces quick action.
2. **Break Tasks into Small Steps**
   Start with a tiny action you can complete quickly. Small wins build momentum and keep you moving fast.
3. **Embrace Imperfection**
   Accept that your first try doesn't have to be perfect. Launch or act "good enough" and improve as you go.

4. **Trust Your Instincts**
   Listen to your gut feeling and act on it. Practice making small decisions based on intuition to build confidence.
5. **Limit Information Intake**
   Don't drown yourself in research. Set a limit on how much info you gather before acting to avoid analysis paralysis.
6. **Use the 2-Minute Rule**
   If a task or decision takes less than 2 minutes, do it immediately instead of postponing it.
7. **Create a Daily "Action List"**
   Write down the top 3 things to do each day and commit to starting them quickly without delay.
8. **Practice "Speed Sprints"**
   Set a timer and challenge yourself to complete tasks or make decisions within a short burst of focused time.
9. **Learn from Mistakes Quickly**
   If you make a mistake, analyse it briefly, then adjust and move on fast. Don't dwell on errors.
10. **Visualize Success Through Speed**
    Before starting, picture yourself acting quickly and achieving results. This mental practice builds your speed mindset.

Speed isn't chaos, it's clarity in motion. It's choosing to act while others are still waiting for the stars to align. Success doesn't come to those who hesitate; it rewards those who dare to begin. Like Bruce Lee said, *"If you spend too much time thinking about a thing, you'll never get it done."* Walt Disney echoed the truth: *"The way to get started is to quit talking and begin doing."* And in the words of Karen Lamb, *"A year from now, you may wish you had started today."* So start now even if it's messy, even if it's small. Set time limits, trust your instincts, and get comfortable being imperfect. Make mistakes fast, learn faster, and keep showing up. As Grandma would put it, *"Child, don't stand there polishing your shoes if you're too scared to take a step. Scuffed shoes still get you there."* The world doesn't need your perfect plan, it needs your first bold move. Speed isn't just an advantage, it's your proof that you're serious.

XXVII
The Unshakeable Power of Confidence

"With confidence, you have won before you have started." – *Marcus Garvey*
Or as I like to say, twirk like you own the place, even if your knees are cracking.

Now listen, sugar, confidence ain't just some sparkly thing you find in the clearance bin next to self-help books and overpriced candles. It's the starter pistol of your whole dang life. Every wild dream, every bold move, every time you chose to stand tall when the world told you to shrink? Yep, that was confidence whispering, *"Get up, baby. You've got this."*

And let me tell you something confidence isn't about being the loudest in the room. (Though I *am*, and unapologetically so.) It's about being the one who knows she belongs there, even if her lipstick is a little smudged and she's wearing mismatched socks. It's not about being fearless, *honey, please!* Fear still knocks on my door every Tuesday, but confidence is the reason I don't answer.

"Feel the fear and do it anyway."- Susan Jeffers .You better believe I at this age still do, sometimes wearing heels.

People get it all twisted, thinking confidence shows up *after* the glowup, the success, or the applause. No, darling. It's the other way around. You become magnetic because you dared to believe you were enough *before* anyone else said so. According to psychology professor Amy Cuddy, *"Don't fake it till you make it. Fake it till you become it."* And let me tell you, half the people you admire are out here wingin' it with great posture. Let me put it plainly: confidence is not arrogance. Arrogance walks in yelling, "Look at me!" Confidence walks in and people do. It's a quiet light. The kind that doesn't need to scream to be seen. It's how you carry yourself when everything around you is wobbling.

"Nothing can dim the light which shines from within."- Maya Angelou . Confidence is the sparkle in your eye when life throws curveballs, and you still swing. It's the grace in your step when your heart's a little broken, but your spirit's still dancing. Heck, it's even in the way I talk back to my mirror when it tries to get smart with me in the morning. And you know what the best part is? Confidence is contagious. Walk into a room believing you're worthy, and watch how it changes the air, the people, the energy. Even my 30 year old boyfriend started moisturizing because of my glow up. That's influence, baby. So next time that little voice in your head says you're not enough, you just channel me, your sassy, wrinkled, wildly fabulous inner Grandma and say: Watch me.

Confidence: The Inner Radiance

As told by your slightly inappropriate, wildly inspiring Grandma who has survived war, heartbreak, bad fringes, and worse men, and still walks like she owns every room.

Honey, let me tell you something right now, no amount of makeup, muscles, filters, or fancy lighting can outshine the glow of real self-confidence. You could slap on all the contour in Sephora and still feel invisible if you don't like who's staring back at you in the mirror.

Confidence? That's an *inside job, sugar.* It's not about how others see you. It's about how you see you.

A truly confident soul stands out not because they're trying to, but because they carry themselves like they matter. And when you believe you matter, people start believing it too. That's the magic. It's a quiet power. Like walking into a room and not saying a single word, yet the air shifts. That's presence. That's confidence.

Again repeating what Maya said "Nothing can dim the light which shines from within." And baby, if Maya said it, you better stitch it on a pillow and believe it. People are drawn to secure energy, not perfection. We've all met those folks who walk around puffed-up like roosters in a windstorm, loud and shiny but deeply fragile underneath. That's not confidence, that's noise. Real confidence is calm. It's that unshakable "I've survived some stuff and I'm still standing" kind of calm.

Now, don't get it twisted, Grandma wasn't born like this. I wasn't always walking around with red lipstick and wisdom dripping from my pearls. Nope. I was the girl sitting in the back of the class, chewing on my hair, praying no one would look my way. Wanna know the kind of stuff I heard growing up?

"You're ugly. Dumb. Unlovable."

And don't even get me started on that boy, 10 years older, thinking he was some kind of Greek God, looked at me in 8th grade and said, *"Everyone in your school looks cute, why do you look like this?"* Bless his soul, he is dead now . Let me tell you something, sweetheart, that man probably forgot what he said by dinner. But I remembered it for years. But that sentence stuck to my bones. And it hurt. Bad.

But guess what?

I didn't sink. I rose. Not like a phoenix. No, that's too glamorous. I rose like biscuits in the oven, slow, sometimes lopsided, but always rising.

I faced my fears like a one woman army:

• Public speaking? Did it with shivering hands and sweaty pits.

• Moving to a new city? Terrified. Did it anyway.

• Writing my story? Scared. But I knew it could set someone else free.

"You gain strength, courage, and confidence by every experience in which you really stop to look fear in the face." – Eleanor Roosevelt

And Lord knows I stared fear down so many times, I'm on a first name basis with it.

I stopped waiting to be perfect. As Grandma always said, 'Perfect is a myth, probably cooked up by someone so scared of real power, they hoped folks would stay too busy chasing flaws to realize they were born to change the world.' I chose instead to embrace the raw, broken, awkward, brilliant mess that is me.

Do I still have days where I feel like I'm not enough? Heck yes. But you know what? I don't unpack and live there anymore. I let the feeling visit, then I kick it out like I do my ex-husbands.

"Confidence is not 'they will like me.' It's 'I'll be fine if they don't.'" - Christina Grimmie

These days, I look in the mirror and don't cry anymore. I stand tall, not because I changed how I look, but because I changed how I see myself. That, my dear, is the real glow up.

"I am not what happened to me. I am what I choose to become." – Carl Jung

And I choose to become the most fabulous, healed, unbothered version of me.

So here's my advice: Stop shrinking. Stop apologizing. Stop waiting to feel ready.

You already have everything you need inside you, you just have to trust it. And if your knees are cracking, let them. Walk in anyway.

Root Confidence in the Inner Self- The Real Magic

Now listen close, darling. If your confidence depends on your looks, your latest trophy, or what Aunt Munima thinks, honey, you're building your castle on sand. That kind of confidence wobbles like a toddler learning to walk. But when you root it deep inside, in that quiet, fierce knowing of who you are it becomes tougher.

Here's a secret the stars don't want you to know: those people you're always looking up to? They don't have some magic wand you missed out on. Nope. Their power is just plain old belief, the kind you carry inside when you stop handing your power away. Because, honey, *"You give others their power when you think they're better than you."* And that's a gift nobody should get for free.

Eleanor Roosevelt was a wise lady when she said, *"No one can make you feel inferior without your consent."* Think about that. Nobody can sneak in and steal your sparkle unless you open the door and let 'em. So lock that door tight and keep your crown polished.

Confidence is like fire, not the kind that burns down your kitchen, but the kind that warms your soul and lights up everyone around you. Like a phoenix rising from the ashes, a confident person knows the flames are just part of the story, the real magic is in the rising.

Sure, you'll have your off days. Those sneaky voices might still try whispering their lies. But once you build your confidence on the inside? They don't stand a chance. You'll just smile, remember your worth, and say, *"Not today."*

Self-Efficacy : Believe before you see it

Now listen here, sweetheart, back in 1977, a clever fella named Albert Bandura came along and put a fancy name on something Grandma always knew deep down: if you believe you can do something, even just a little bit, you're already halfway there. He called it *self-efficacy*, which is just a ten dollar way of saying "believing in your own magic." What it really means is trusting yourself to figure things out. You don't have to have all the answers before you start; you just have to believe you're the kind of person who'll find them. When you truly believe in yourself, you try harder. When life knocks you down on your behind, and oh, it will you get back up, shake off the dust, and try again. That's how you get better, stronger, and more likely to win the next round.

As Henry Ford wisely said, "Whether you think you can or you think you can't, you're right." He wasn't just flapping his gums, either. Your brain is a powerful little drama queen. If you tell it, "I can't," it'll start shutting doors faster than you can say, "Oops." But if you say, "I've got this," your brain will start looking for ways to help you win. It's like having your own personal cheerleader, but only if you feed it the right lines. Grandma likes to think of confidence like growing tomatoes you gotta water it, talk nice to it, and trust that even if it looks small today, with time, it'll bear fruit. But if you don't believe it'll grow, well, you won't even plant the seed. So go ahead, love, believe in yourself, even if your voice shakes and your knees creak. That's how all good things start.

Confidence- Competence Loop:

Now, listen here, sugar, confidence doesn't just show up once you've mastered something like magic. Nope, it actually grows *while* you're stumbling, fumbling, and figuring things out. It's what the smarty-pants call the *Confidence-Competence Loop*. Here's how it works: you try something new, maybe you're all mess at first, like trying to bake a cake without burning down the kitchen. But you keep at it, and before long, you survive the mess, maybe you even get a little taste of success. Your brain files that win away like a little gold star, and suddenly you feel braver the next time you try. So you keep at it, and bit by bit, you get better, and that makes you more confident, which makes you keep trying. It's a beautiful cycle, sugar. Take J.K. Rowling, for example, the woman behind Harry Potter. She faced rejection after rejection but kept writing anyway. She said, "Rock bottom became the solid foundation on which I rebuilt my life." Science backs this, too: practicing even when you're not perfect lights up the parts of your brain that boost your confidence and motivation. So, as Grandma says, "You don't wait to feel ready, baby, you get ready by doing." So go ahead, stumble, fall, and get back up, because that's how confidence is born, one brave step at a time.

Body Language:

Now listen up, sweet pea, your body talks *way* louder than your mouth ever could. Harvard's very own Amy Cuddy, dropped a real truth bomb in her famous TED Talk about something called "power posing." That's just a fancy way of saying, stand tall and proud like you're Wonder Woman for just two minutes. Sounds silly? Well, science says it actually works! When you hold yourself like a boss, your body starts pumping out more testosterone, that's the hormone that whispers, "Hey, you got this!" and it dials down cortisol, the nasty little stress hormone that makes you feel like a scaredy cat. Amy's research found that 86% of folks who did this power pose before an interview felt way more confident, and guess what? They were rated higher and got hired more often. Think of it like walking into a room with your head high and shoulders back, like you're carrying a secret no one else knows but you do. Remember what Coco Chanel said, "The most courageous act is still to think for yourself. Aloud." Your posture is your first loud "I'm here" before you even say a word. So stand tall, walk proud, and let your body do the talking.

The Impostor Syndrome Paradox: When Doubt and Confidence Dance

Alright, dear, be ready Grandma's got some real talk for you. That little voice inside your head, the one that whispers, *"Who do you think you are?"* that's called Impostor Syndrome. And don't you dare think you're alone with it. According to the brilliant psychologists Dr. Pauline Clance and Dr. Suzanne Imes, over 70% of people wrestle with this sneaky feeling. That means most folks you admire, from the highest achievers to your next-door neighbor have faced this doubt. It's like showing up to a fancy party feeling like you're wearing a costume while everyone else has on a tuxedo.

But here's what Grandma wants you to remember: **doubting yourself doesn't mean you lack confidence.** It means you're awake enough to see your own imperfections, brave enough to feel the fear, and smart enough to keep going anyway. It's the difference between stumbling and staying down.

Take Maya Angelou, that fierce soul who told us, *"I have written eleven books, but each time I think, 'Uh-oh, they're going to find out now. I've run a game on everybody.'"* Or Michelle Obama, who once admitted to feeling out of place, yet pushed herself forward anyway, saying, *"Just try new things. Don't be afraid. Step out of your comfort zones and soar, all right?"* These legends didn't get rid of their doubts they chose to keep moving even when their hearts shook.

Science backs this too. Studies show that impostor feelings often come from high personal standards and the fear of failure. But guess what? That fear, when faced head on, fuels growth. It sharpens you like a whetstone shapes a blade. The real trick is not to silence your doubt completely but to make it a quiet companion instead of the loud boss in your mind.

Remember what Suzy Kassem said, *"Doubt kills more dreams than failure ever will."* Don't let that doubt choke your dreams before you even start dancing with them. Let it whisper, but never let it roar.

So next time your inner critic tries to steal the spotlight, Grandma says give it a wink, pat it on the head, and say, *"Thanks for the concern, but I've got this."* Because confidence isn't about never doubting, it's about choosing to rise in spite of it.

The Mirror Effect: Self-Talk & Neuroplasticity

Now listen here, sweetheart, confidence isn't something you're just born with, like your eye color . Nope! Confidence is like a muscle, you gotta work it, feed it, and love it every single day. And guess what? Your brain is the boss behind the scenes, quietly rewiring itself every time you say something nice about yourself. That's called neuroplasticity, a fancy way of saying your brain is as flexible as a gymnast and can change for the better, no matter how old you are.

Grandma likes to say it this way: *"Tell yourself you're a queen/king long enough, and your brain starts building you a damn throne."* When you talk kindly to yourself, when you say, *"I got this,"* or *"I'm enough,"* your brain starts making new paths, stronger paths, that tell your whole body and soul, *"Hey, she's/he's the real deal."* It's like planting seeds, the more you water them with good words and love, the bigger and stronger that garden of confidence grows.

Take a look at people like Oprah Winfrey. She's shared how positive affirmations helped her rise from tough beginnings to become one of the most powerful voices in the world. She once said, *"The greatest discovery of all time is that a person can change their future by merely changing their attitude."* That's neuroplasticity, baby changing your attitude, rewiring your brain, changing your life. Science backs it too: studies show that when you practice positive self-talk, visualize yourself succeeding, and treat yourself with compassion, your confidence gets a real boost, and anxiety starts to pack its bags. It's like training your brain to be your biggest fan instead of your harshest critic.

So next time you catch yourself in the mirror, Grandma wants you to smile and say, *"You're doing good, sugar. Keep going."* Because every kind word you whisper to yourself is a brick in the palace you're building to the beautiful you.

Daily Confidence Boosters

1. **Give Yourself a Sassy Nickname**
   Start your day by calling yourself something fabulous. "Good morning, Queen!" or "Hello, Rockstar!" Say it out loud like you own it. Because if you don't hype yourself up, who will?
2. **Dance Like Nobody's Watching (But Hope They Are)**
   Put on your favorite tune and shake what your mama gave you for at least 2 minutes. Doesn't matter if you look silly, confidence is born in moments like these. Plus, a little wiggle wakes up your happy hormones.
3. **Talk to Yourself Like You're Your Own Bestie**
   If your best friend showed up feeling down, you'd lift her up with jokes, hugs, and killer compliments. So do that for yourself! Grandma says, "Be your own hype squad, darling. And make it loud."
4. **Wear Your "Power Piece"**
   Maybe it's that bold lipstick, those crazy earrings, or your favorite funky socks. Put on something that makes you feel like you just walked off a runway, even if you're just taking out the trash.
5. **Flip the Script on 'Oops' Moments**
   Messed up your coffee order? Tripped on your own feet? Laugh it off and instead of getting embarrassed turn it to a style moment!" Confidence loves a good sense of humor.
6. **Pretend You're Meeting Your Crush (Even If It's Just You)**
   Walk into any room like you're about to dazzle someone special. Shoulders back, smile wide, and sparkle in your eye. Grandma calls this "strut therapy."
7. **Give a Compliment to a Stranger**
   Spread the confidence love! Tell someone they have a great smile or rockin' shoes. It's like giving your confidence a little turbo boost kindness is a power move.
8. Ditch the Crutch and Show Up as You Are

Pick one thing you rely on to "feel confident", maybe it's your fancy shoes, your perfect hair, or that secret phrase you repeat in your head. Now, *leave it behind for a day.* Go out there without your usual confidence crutch and face the world just as you are. Scary? Sure. But that's where real confidence grows in showing up, imperfections and all, and realizing the world doesn't fall apart. Grandma's tip: *"Confidence isn't in what you wear or say, it's in knowing you're enough, with or without the extras."* I am at this age still *trying to go out without my red lipstick.*

Remember, honey, confidence doesn't come from having everything perfectly lined up. As Eleanor Roosevelt wisely said, *"No one can make you feel inferior without your consent."* Your power lies in owning your story and loving yourself through all the bumps and bruises, like Brené Brown puts it, *"Owning our story and loving ourselves through that process is the bravest thing that we'll ever do."* It takes courage to face your fears, but as Eleanor reminds us, *"You gain strength, courage, and confidence by every experience in which you really stop to look fear in the face."* So believe you can, because like Theodore Roosevelt said, *"Believe you can and you're halfway there."* Confidence, baby, is knowing you're enough, right now, just as you are and that, my dear, is the greatest freedom of all.

The Cosmic Perspective – Living Beyond Yourself Purpose, divine alignment, and embracing the mystery of life.

XXVIII

The Future Is Calling You Back

"The distinction between past, present and future is only a stubbornly persistent illusion."

-Albert Einstein

Sugar we often live life like a straight line: from yesterday to today, from now to tomorrow. Everything we do seems to be based on the past shaping the present, the present building the future. We look backward to find meaning and forward to find hope. But what if that entire perception is not just limited, but fundamentally flawed?

What if the future is not just a destination but a cause?

What if your future self is reaching back through time, whispering wisdom into your soul, igniting your intuition, and guiding your every step through divine echoes?

This is not just poetic optimism. It's not wishful thinking or mystical abstraction. It's a growing idea in quantum physics and a powerful metaphor in personal transformation. It is the strange, powerful concept of retrocausality, the idea that the future can influence the past.

It might sound wild. But then again, isn't all growth wild?

The Quantum Clue: Future Shapes the Now

In the weird, wonderful world of quantum mechanics, scientists have encountered experiments where the result of a choice made in the present appears to affect the behavior of particles in the past. This isn't science fiction, it's science fact.

The "Delayed Choice Quantum Eraser" experiment, for instance, shows that a decision made after a particle has been detected can still change how that particle behaved before it was measured. As if the future had the audacity to rewrite history.

Mind-bending? Absolutely. But maybe we're looking at a mirror of how life works, too. Maybe your most aligned, fulfilled, healed self is already "out there," like a lighthouse, sending beams of intention backward through time, nudging you to choose better, rise faster, and trust deeper.

Maybe destiny is less about fate and more about a future memory calling you home.

Faith Is a Form of Retrocausality

We often talk about faith like it's blind. But real faith? It sees the future so clearly that it begins to reshape the present. It rearranges your priorities, strengthens your resolve, and rewrites the narrative you live by.

"Faith is the substance of things hoped for, the evidence of things not seen."- Hebrews 11:1

When you act in faith, you are living under the influence of your future. You're not reacting to the past; you're responding to a higher, greater future that already exists in your imagination, your spirit, your calling. Your future self is feeding you glimpses of what could be, asking you: Will you walk toward me?

What Would Change If You Believed Your Future Self Already Existed?

If the most powerful, radiant, peaceful version of you is already real in some timeline , what would you do differently today? What would you stop tolerating? What would you start honoring? You wouldn't delay. You wouldn't doubt. You wouldn't keep repeating the cycles that keep you small. You would become magnetic to alignment. You would start trusting your instincts, not because they come from nowhere, but because they come from there. From the future.

From the wiser, bolder, deeply awakened version of you who already crossed the fire and made it to the other side.

How to Tap Into Retrocausality

This isn't just philosophy. It can be a daily practice. You can start living today as if your best future has already happened, and your only task is to catch up.

1. Speak from the End.

Speak about your life from the place of destiny. Say, "I am becoming" not "I hope to." Use your words to echo what your future has already declared.

Your language plants seeds in the soil of time.

2. Walk Like the Healed You.

Stop waiting to be confident, calm, successful, or happy. Ask, "How would that version of me live?" Then do it. Today. Dress like them. Speak like them. Make decisions like them.

3. Listen to the Echo.

Your gut feelings. Your dreams. That nudge that says, "Apply anyway," "Let go of them," or "You were made for more", these are not random. They're signals from your future self, calling you upward.

4. Rewrite with Purpose.

Start looking at past pain through the lens of what it built in you. Your struggles weren't just obstacles; they were classrooms. Maybe you had to go through that heartbreak so you could teach others how to heal. Maybe the delay was divine design.

Retrocausality in History and Humanity

Think of great inventors, leaders, and artists. They often speak of "seeing" the vision before it ever happened.

Steve Jobs said:

"You can't connect the dots looking forward; you can only connect them looking backward. But you have to trust that the dots will somehow connect in your future."

But what if the dots were already connected in the future? What if that connection sends a ripple backwards, guiding your hand, your thoughts, your yeses and your noes?

Think of Martin Luther King Jr., who declared, "I have a dream," not as a wish but as a future memory. His speech echoed from a world that did not yet exist, but it shaped millions of decisions that built toward it.

The Butterfly Effect: Small Choices, Huge Ripples

There is a theory in chaos science called the Butterfly Effect, which suggests that the smallest of actions , like a butterfly flapping its wings in Brazil can create a tornado in Texas. It's the idea that tiny choices in the present can echo into massive outcomes in the future.

But retrocausality flips this on its head. What if the tornado in the future is the reason the butterfly flaps its wings today? What if your success in five years is the very reason you choose to stay disciplined, kind, and committed now?

This is how greatness begins: not in grand gestures, but in quiet decisions that ripple across time.You become who you're meant to be by honoring the small voice from the future that says, "Don't quit. Keep going. You matter."

You Are Already in the Future's Hands

Every desire you have for growth, freedom, and peace is not just born from pain or lack. It's born from your future self , someone who is already living those outcomes calling you forward.

What if you began to live your life like a prophecy in motion?

What if your job was not to "create" a better life, but to align with the one that already exists?

What if you stopped asking, "What do I need to become?" and started asking, "What do I need to remember?"

Because perhaps the healed, divine, powerful version of you is not waiting to be made... but waiting to be met.

Let the Future Pull You Home

You are not stuck.

You are not late.

You are not too broken or too far gone.

You are standing in the middle of a timeline that already knows your victory.

So the next time you feel that pull inside, that voice saying, "There's more, you are more" don't silence it. That's not fantasy. That's your future.

Let it shape your now.

Let it guide your choices.

Let it rewrite your past with purpose.

Because the future is calling you back.

And this time you're ready to answer.

XXIX

We Never Meet Anyone by Accident

Darling some people walk into our lives like whispers gentle, soft, and almost unnoticed just like my boyfriend. Others arrive like storms shaking us, challenging us, forever changing the landscape of who we are like Munima. Even Munima is important, if not for her, I would have missed most of my smiles. And yet, none of them are accidents.

Every single person we meet serves a purpose.

They come as a lesson, a blessing, a mirror, or a catalyst.

Whether they stay for a moment, a season, or a lifetime, their presence was written into our story before we even knew how to read it.

The Divine Timing of Connection

Have you ever met someone and instantly felt, *Where were you all this time?* As though their absence had left an invisible space in your world? And yet, somehow, they arrived at the exact moment you were ready for them.

"When the student is ready, the teacher will appear." – Lao Tzu

There is no such thing as "too late" in divine timing. The universe doesn't rush and it doesn't delay. It delivers exactly what you need when your heart, your mind, your soul are aligned to receive it. Sometimes, people arrive when you are at your lowest, your heart bruised and tired.

They become the unexpected healing the warm presence that reminds you that joy still exists.

Others show up just as you are stepping into your power, and they push you even further, challenging you to grow, expand, evolve.

"Every person you meet knows something you don't. Learn from them."- H. Jackson Brown Jr.

The Mirror of Every Soul

Carl Jung once said,

"Everything that irritates us about others can lead us to an understanding of ourselves."

That's because everyone you meet is a mirror, reflecting back parts of you that you might not have seen, acknowledged, or embraced.

- The ones who frustrate you often mirror your own insecurities or unhealed wounds.
- The ones who inspire you reflect the greatness already alive within you.
- The ones who love you deeply show you how to love yourself again.

What you admire in others is waiting to be awakened in you.

What triggers you in others is asking to be healed in you.

"We don't see things as they are, we see them as we are." – Anaïs Nin

Relationships are sacred assignments. Every person is either helping you move forward or holding up a mirror to show you what's holding you back.

The Red Thread of Fate

There's a beautiful Chinese proverb that says:

"An invisible red thread connects those who are destined to meet, regardless of time, place, or circumstance. The thread may stretch or tangle, but it will never break."

Some meetings feel like accidents, but they're actually reunions.

When you meet someone and feel like you've known them forever, that's not chemistry, that's recognition.

Your soul is remembering another soul it has loved before. Soulmates aren't just lovers. They can be friends, mentors, even strangers who spark something eternal inside you.

Even the painful ones had a purpose. Not every soul comes to comfort you. Some come to crack you open.

To challenge you.

To test your boundaries.

To trigger your growth.

Some people come into our lives to awaken us. They serve their purpose and then they leave. And that's okay.

The Lessons Hidden in Pain

Not all connections feel good but all are sacred.

- The heartbreak? Taught you boundaries.
- The betrayal? Showed you your worth.
- The abandonment? Made you strong.
- The silence? Taught you to hear your own voice.

"What hurts you, blesses you. Darkness is your candle." – Rumi
Painful people are not mistakes. They are sacred sandpaper, smoothing out the rough edges of who you are becoming. They are the hard chapters, yes but without them, you wouldn't reach the breakthrough that follows.

"Sometimes the people who hurt you the most are the ones who teach you the most."

The Butterfly Effect of a Single Encounter
Have you ever looked back and realized how one person changed your entire life?

- One kind word from a stranger on your worst day.
- One mentor who saw your light when you only saw shadows.
- One friend who believed in you and reminded you to keep going.
- One love who broke you open and made you feel again.

"Sometimes the smallest step in the right direction ends up being the biggest step of your life." – Naeem Callaway
These are not little things.These are moments that altered your trajectory forever.

That's the **butterfly effect**, one conversation, one meeting, one glance that ripples across your entire life. *Sometimes people don't realize the impact they have on someone else's life.*

You Are That Person for Someone, Too
We often think about how others affect us.
But have you ever paused to consider who **you** have been for someone else?

- Maybe you were the only person who listened when they needed to speak.
- Maybe your smile gave them a reason to believe again.
- Maybe your honesty helped them face the truth.
- Maybe your presence reminded them they weren't alone.

"Be the kind of person who makes others feel seen, heard, and loved." – Brené Brown

You're not just walking through life; you're walking into people's stories.

You're the whisper they needed.

The encouragement they prayed for.

The spark that reignited something they thought they lost.

"Your life is your message to the world. Make sure it's inspiring."- Lorrin L. Lee

Live Like Nothing Is Random

So, live as though nothing is random.

Love as though every soul you meet matters, because they do.

Cherish the joy, forgive the pain, and honor the presence of every person who crossed your path.

"There are no accidents... there is only some purpose that we haven't yet understood."-Deepak Chopra

Some people walk beside you.

Some walk away.

Some walk in just to teach you how to walk alone.

Let them all be part of your becoming.

Let Every Goodbye Be a Blessing

When the time comes to part ways, do it with grace. Some people aren't meant to stay forever, they're meant to awaken something within you, then move on.

"Don't cry because it's over. Smile because it happened." – Dr. Seuss

Bless them for the role they played. Release them with gratitude. And continue becoming the person you're meant to be.

Final Reminder: The Sacredness of Every Soul

Baby, there are no accidental meetings. No chance encounters. No "just happened to be there" moments. The universe is too intentional. And your story is too sacred. *Every person in your life is aligned to your purpose.* So walk with eyes wide open. Speak love. Show up fully. Forgive deeply and remember, every soul you meet is a divine assignment, a spiritual message, a cosmic mirror.

Honor them.

Learn from them.

And when it's time, let them go in peace

"The future influences the present just as much as the past."- Friedrich Nietzsch

The End

Well, here we are, sweetheart, the last page. And if you've made it this far, let me be the first to say: Damn, I'm proud of you.

You started this journey in a fog, confused, tired, maybe even a little broken. But baby, look at you now. You kept turning the pages even when your hands were shaky. You stared down some hard truths. You opened old wounds and started applying medicine. That's not easy. That's holy work.

You didn't just read about change, you danced with it, wrestled with it, and I hope somewhere along the way, you fell in love with who you're becoming. That mess you thought would swallow you whole? You turned it into meaning. Those cracks in your heart? You've filled them with gold. That light you thought you lost? It's beaming now, don't you dare dim it again for anyone.

"The wound is the place where the Light enters you."- Rumi

I always told you, sugar, this book ain't about fixing you. You were never broken. This was about finding you, the real you, beneath the roles and regrets and rules you were taught to follow. And if all you did was catch a glimpse of that person then mission damn near accomplished.

But don't stop here. Don't you dare close this book and go back to shrinking just to fit into other people's stories. Write your own now. Boldly. Loudly. Kindly. And when the storms come again (because oh, honey, they will), don't panic. You've got anchors now, truth, faith, stillness, self love, and Grandma's sass woven into your bones.

Life won't always make sense, and people won't always play fair. But you? You've got something better than control, you've got clarity. And clarity, darling, that's power.

Now, before you go off chasing dreams and setting fires in the best possible way, let me leave you with this:
If ever you forget who you are, reread this book. Not for the words, but for the reflection.

You are not the pain that tried to bury you.
You are the bloom that rose anyway.

"And the day came when the risk to remain tight in a bud was more painful than the risk it took to blossom."- Anaïs Nin

So go on, baby live loud, love big, give generously, and rest when you need to. The world needs your kind of real. And when it all feels too much again? Just remember what Grandma always says:

"You've already survived 100% of your worst days, sugar. You've got this. And I've got you."

"You don't have to see the whole staircase, just take the first step." -Martin Luther King Jr.

With every ounce of love I've got,
Grandma Sniffa